TICKET TO
HEAVEN

TICKET TO
HEAVEN

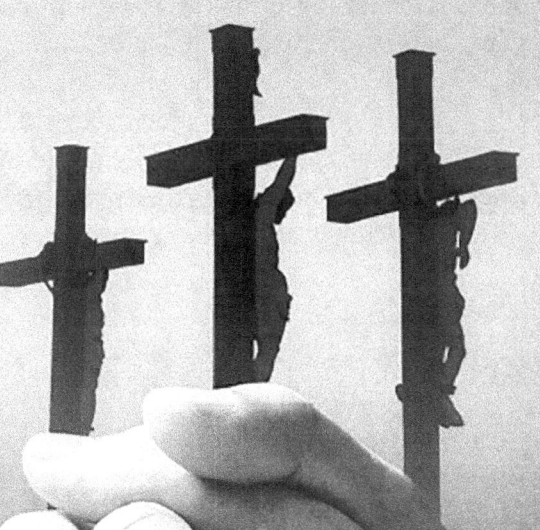

TERRY B. RICHESIN

AKPress
ILLUMINATING IDEAS
EMPOWERING VOICES

ARPress
45 Dan Road Suite 5
Canton MA 02021
Hotline: 1(888) 821-0229
Fax: 1(508) 545-7580

Ordering Information:

Quantity sales. Special discounts are available on quantity purchases by corporations, associations, and others. For details, contact the publisher at the address above.

Printed in the United States of America.

ISBN-13:   Softcover   979-8-89330-738-2

             eBook   979-8-89330-739-9

Library of Congress Control Number: 2024902828

Table of Contents

DEDICATED

To all lost souls. May these words comfort and guide you to JESUS, our SAVIOR.

Father, My Serenity

Condensation I feel sponging out of me. I seem to recall some of life's simplicity. Yeah it's only reality. Hardships are indigenous, rare to avoid. Actions speak in multitudes. Words at times just a ploy.

A blanket of serenity, solace to me. The one who is my refuge my salvation for me. Ocean waves rise only to fall in a clash. Clouds so extremely high but it is You my JESUS, you are my life. I adore Thee with all Thine soul. I scamper in strides just to know.

My salvation, SAVIOR, Father I see. Ocean waves cannot contain me. I owe you absolutely everything, for You are my serenity. Life is awkward it has its highs, oh and it contains its lows. Life's essence of camouflage just for show.

Man is influenced by situations that only JESUS beholds. A chameleon that equips its traits only to falsely emulate to its foes. Just be yourself, overwhelm yourself with unity. Father reach out for me, Father my serenity.

Just Believe

This just in so brace yourself to something tight. Strap
yourself in my friend. Faith is what you need. Listen to
your heart and just believe. Our LORD is to return once again
to claim HIS faithful and worthy children. Faith is what you need.
JESUS is whom you seek. Tears will inevitably fall.
CHRIST will gracefully catch them all.

So step into HIS mercy, oh HIS love. Raise your hands
honestly. You will see. Oh my friend just believe in our
MAJESTY, just believe.

The day will take place when love will eliminate all hate.
Our SAVIOR will come to claim all that is whole. Just believe
that HE can save your soul. One more visit, one last time.
Just believe that in the end it's JESUS you'll find.

Do you see? Do you want to be free? Take HIS hand and Just believe.

What Do You Tell A Child?

What do you tell a child with eyes full of tears? What do you tell a child who's only been on earth for six years? What do you tell a child when they ask why daddy? Why did mommy have to die? What is the truth? Why daddy why?

What do you tell a child when their world comes crashing down? What do you tell a child when all you see is a frown? What do you tell a child that seeks reasons why people die? What do you tell a child who just wants to know why?

I tell my child with tears falling down: Mommy is in Heaven looking down, oh down on you. She is with you in spirit, forever day and night. Just because you do not see her does not mean she's out of sight. Mommy is in heaven with the angels. She had a job to do. She is helping GOD prepare a place in Heaven for me and you.

Pray every night and day. Do what you can. Remember GOD can always use a helping hand.

One Day Just To Be

One man took life just to die. HE left us with love and salvation.

One man saved all with redemption, pure love and grace.
Is it any wonder why one day I just want to be in YOUR glory, with you FATHER to be safe?

One day just to be out of all this. Faithfully, willingly spending eternity in nothing but pure bliss. One day just to be in all YOUR glory. Oh I want to be free with YOU; just to be.

One man lay down for us HIS life on the cross. Now a spirit shining HIS Holy Light for the lost. One day just to be out of all this. Faithfully, willingly spending eternity in nothing but pure bliss. Take me; take me out of all this.

Sign Your Name Here

If you ever feel, feel left out in the cold. Just know, know that you are not alone. If you ever shout why now? Why me? Just take a second and drop to your knees.

Sign your name here, sign with a tear. If you ever feel helpless and so out of place, well just know that there are others running the same race, all at a different pace. Some fast, some slow, some high, some low.

Sign your name here if you're full of doubt. Sign your name here if just simply you want out.

If you feel in your heart that JESUS is the way and you just want to keep the Devil at bay, you have come to the right place. JESUS knows your face and every tear.
Put your faith in him and sign your name here.

Take This Book

Take this book. Take it, take a look. Take this book
I give it to you. Read all you can. See what CHRIST went
through. Open it up, look inside. Read how our JESUS lived
and also how HE died. Take this book from my hand. Don't
just skim through pages, try to understand. Read every
page, read every story. Don't put it down even when some
pages get quite gory.

So the story goes with every page turned. So HIS Glory
glows with every candle burned. We are to shine our light,
burn it bright so everyone can see. Put a smile on our
SAVIOR'S face and spell victory.

So take this, more than a good book. Oh and please take
more than just a look. Read HIS words, keep them in your
heart. And just know with HIS pure love you will never part.
Take this book from my hand. Read it, read it
when you can.

Have I Told You?

Have I told YOU that I love and appreciate YOU? Well I do!
Oh and have I said to YOU that one day and only one way
that I long to see YOU? Oh I only hope that there are many
and not just a few to be in YOUR open arms and to be
with YOU.

YOU are our MASTER, our CREATOR, the only ONE. I can't say
enough. YOU gave up for us YOUR only SON and for that our
work for YOU is never done!

Have I told YOU that YOU'RE an AWESOME GOD and ever so
forgiving? And that I am living, living for YOU. But do not
forget I only work for YOU. Well I do! Let's get to work our
job is incomplete. We long for the day we meet!

Believe and Be Free

Do you feel alone? Are you tired now? Are you at the point? Do you just want to lay your body down? Are you weeping while you sleep? Your hands empty and nothing to keep?

Are you all alone? Have you had enough? Would you like to know and would you like to see? Would you like to feel alive? Take my hand and follow me.

Oh surrender, believe and be free. Have you heard of JESUS? Can't you feel HIS love? HIS presence has no limit.

Can you feel HIS Holy SPIRIT? Do you see the Truth? It is only HE that can save you. Are you all alone? Have you had enough? Would you like to know? Would you like to see? Would you like to feel alive? Take my hand and follow me.

Oh surrender, believe and be free. Next time you feel alone, believe in JESUS and be free.

Picking Up The Pieces

I think about all that YOU are. How amazing it is to know YOU and every awesome thing YOU do. I keep that one promise in my heart and in my soul. That certain place YOU tell me I will someday go. Somehow, some way YOU guide us through every day. YOU'RE always the one picking up the pieces, mending us together over and over every passing day. Oh JESUS, you're always picking up the pieces in every way.

YOU do for us, all what it takes. When life seems to feel so upside down and incomplete, YOU fill in the missing pieces. You will turn it completely around and keep us sound. If ever I feel lost, oh I know with YOUR Mercy I will always be found.

Oh JESUS CHRIST you're the One, GOD'S true SON. If ever we feel weary and stumble in the dark, YOU'RE always picking up the pieces. That's just who YOU are. YOU'RE always picking up the pieces. YOU are the way to that place of true bliss. Only YOU can fill in each blank space with every true piece YOU make fit.

Thank You LORD for picking up the pieces. Mending me together every passing day. Thank You Dear LORD for leading the way.

Abundantly Mine

I find myself simply out of place. Really doesn't matter
what steps I trace. Only You can take them and point them
in place. At those times of doubt and sinful mind I can lay my
load on YOU. Seek and I shall find.

Oh my LORD, YOU are abundantly mine. Temptations will
mirror to all, every mind, all of mankind. Even if I feel like
I am found, oh chained in shackles I know if I speak YOUR
name that there is not one thing I can't tackle.

For YOU are my Glory, my Tabernacle. My soul and YOU
combined. Salvation, Mercy all refined. YOU are, YOU are
abundantly mine. Euphoric bliss that is what YOU bring.
Oh Thank You LORD JESUS. With YOU I will never lag
behind. For I can call YOU my own. YOU, oh
YOU are abundantly mine.

Waiting

I know I won't live forever. I am aware of the fact. Tell me
to move for you LORD. Whatever it takes I'm ready to act.
I'm waiting for more of YOUR love. I'm waiting for YOUR
signs from above.

Oh tell me LORD, I shall wait no more. I love YOU to no
end. Come take me in YOUR merciful arms I want to begin.
Shelter me, Shower me with YOUR love. Show me of this
world when push comes to shove.

I'm waiting, oh waiting but not at a stand still. For I know
that YOU will return. This I know, this I feel. I'm waiting for
more of YOUR love. I'm waiting for YOUR sign from above.
I'm waiting for that ultimate chance, to journey
to the other side.

Oh JESUS, in YOU I do confide. Give me strength to stay one
more day. I'm just waiting, oh waiting to fly away.

Do You?

Is it in you? Oh can you feel it? Can you feel HIM? You must confide everything you're about. You can't, oh you just can't hide. Do you approach any reason unknown to you? Would you? Do you just give up? Just come unglued? Well friend, you are human, I have news for you. Take a breath. Take it slow. Do you feel HIM? Well my friend make it known. Is it in you? Can you feel it?

Do not deny HIM, for HE is our way. There is no document to sign. Just talk to HIM everyday. Bow your head and pray. Do you stray from change? Everything turns. It does not stay the same.

If you know CHRIST, then you know Glorious Heaven is the place to go. Do you feel HIM, oh everywhere? HIS love covers all atmosphere. Do you feel HIM in your heart? Grab hold, reach high and know this: HE will never leave your side.

One Step

I've been thinking about you LORD. Oh more and more, YOU are the only one that really matters. YOU, OH LORD I undoubtedly admire. I am yours. What YOU have done for me, OH JESUS, these tears I shed for THEE.

I just want to take another step, just one step to see YOU. Another step, oh to be with YOU. I want to lift my voice. Sing ever more to rejoice. I can see YOU up on that cross. I can hear YOUR cries. I will take one step further. YOU, OH LORD, I will not deny.

Thank You SAVIOR. Oh Thank You for everything YOU do. I want to take one more step to be, oh to be with you. I want to sing in Heaven, the Golden Gates of Heaven. Oh, I want to go through. Oh, I want to be with YOU. Anything YOU ask me, I will do, oh for YOU.

Speak To Him

Stand up, speak to HIM, from your heart and soul. HE will provide for us the knowledge we must know. I feel so full of HIS true love. Oh stop, just listen to the singing of Angels from above.

Ah the wait to be in HIS honor. I can feel all YOUR love. I know YOU can hear me, Oh FATHER. Come all, pray with me. Kneel down, you will finally see. Let's all speak to HIM. Let's all shout and sing. Come now give HIM everything.

Let us pray. Let us bow. Oh, let us bow to HIM. Oh let, oh let HIM in. HE knows the hearts of every soul. There's no escape, oh there's no place to go. Fear GOD, not man. For GOD is our CREATOR, the very ONE with a plan.

Let HIM in. Speak to HIM. Speak out! Let's sing and shout. Don't hold back. Let it all out. Speak to HIM. Let HIM in. Do it now! Forgive us FATHER, for our sins. Let the love, oh let the love begin. Speak to HIM. Let HIM in.

You Are Forever

It's been a struggle and a half, to reach a place where I've never been before. The steps that I've never taken; too many reasons in the word: procrastinate. Never do what you plan to, until you make the effort.

Oh, YOU are forever. YOU are forever mine and I seek YOU. I trust YOU WITH YOUR light, YOU will bring me to the Truth, YOU are forever. I need to, I want to change. I want to fit my soul, in that sensational place. The streets of gold where Angels, never sing off key. That's where, I want to be. Oh YOU are forever. YOU are forever mine and I seek YOU, I trust YOU.

With YOUR light YOU my KING, will bring me to the Truth. You are forever YOU, forever YOU With YOUR light, YOU my KING, will bring me to YOU are forever YOU.

Trust Your Name

How strong is a circle, without the main component? Trust is the tide, that binds with no end. It all has to start from somewhere, a place to begin. A solid foundation of various proportions. Disruptive forces agitating and frightening off who do not see the Truth.

Maybe way too young for the ultimate answer. Perhaps too immature and far too young. Same old story; a far off different youth with plenty to say. If only they'd call on YOU and trust YOUR name. A society can work effectively as one. Only in a positive way, if they shed their arrogance and trust YOUR name.

The Truth, the Answer is one in the same. There's no riddle, it's all in YOUR precious name. I trust YOUR Holy Name. I trust YOUR name, oh YOUR name.

All I Want

Some say and want all the riches of this world, this life. I simply ask for all of YOUR pure Love. Oh JESUS CHRIST, YOU'RE all I want. YOU'RE all I need. Oh YOU'RE the ONE. Your face, I want to see. YOU'RE all I ask, all I seek. Oh please rid this world of its misery.

Oh it's catastrophes. YOU'RE all I want, all I need. I love YOU for all YOU'VE done for this world of misery.

Some say and want all the power they can gain. I simply just want to be in YOUR presence. Oh I want to touch YOUR face. All I want oh hold me. Oh all I need; Oh JESUS, YOUR face I'll see.

Come, oh come now, rescue me. YOU'RE all I want. Oh SAVIOR, YOU'RE all I need. I am saying,Oh YOU know I am praying, this I plead. Oh YOU'RE all I need.

All I want, all I seek I want to touch YOUR face. I know, yes I know, that YOU Oh JESUS, YOU'RE all I need

In A Flash

Words are often spoke, either near or dear. From the crevice of the heart or from forked tongued twisted evildoers from the endless dark. Atrocious havoc, will and does claim lives of old and young.

Boom! Your life could ultimately end in a flash. Are you willing and eager to spill your blood? What a question. Why don't you ask GOD'S only BEGOTTEN SON?

JESUS took each and every burden one by one. HE carried HIS cross. Any regrets? HE has none.

In a flash a loved one may vanish right in front of your eyes. You may think how can this possibly be right swallowing tears all through the night?

We all have a reason to exist right now. JESUS is to return to us one final time. The power is not for the weak. It does not belong to mankind. The only way to win, to make everything light again: repent of your sins, tell our CHRIST all about them.

In a flash, regrettably just like that anyone we love can evaporate in a flash. And just like that, oh just like that, CHRIST can come down on that day in a flash.

Anytime

Anytime I think of who You are to me this is what I find:
You are so gentle, so filled with love. Oh how blessed You
are. All love within You. You, oh Mother, share and care for
anyone. Oh, what a trait to cherish. To be willing to give and
give. Hey Mother, it's the only way for You to live. May JESUS
heal your every ache. Just believe and I know You do.
Keep on, just keep being You.

P.S. Heaven Awaits!

Just Me

What you see is what you get. No fake image, only a true heart. One full of doubts and emotions on high. Love outdoors: love to look up at the sky. Had very hard times of travesty.

Looking forward, emerging from the misery. I'm just one man. Not really one with a master plan. It's just me, kinda simple full of love and I worship our MASTER, who resides up above.

Oh, I very much love. It's just me, a servant with a task to do. To get one to open their heart, is not easy to do. Everyone has a wall to break through.

Ideas always racing through my head. So I will write them down, neglecting to go to bed. It's just me, one with something to say. Always seeking others to help as much as I possibly can. It's just me, here I am.

A Brand New Man

Say do you know who I am? Do you eagerly remember me? I know what You're foolishly doing here. Drooling, salivating, drumming up some dreadful fears. I resent all that You are. I may still harness a few scars.

Today is bright, all brand new. I open my eyes and eliminate You. I knew You once, but never again. To me, You were too diabolical, hardly a friend.

Time has passed, rightfully so. You're my dead skin, I must now let go. Do You eagerly remember me? Say, do you know who I am?

In prayer, I ask for forgiveness from my LORD JESUS. In turn I stand. A brand new man.

A Touch Of Heaven

Imagine if you will a place of Glory, of pure bliss. All we have to do is accept YOU, Oh LORD JESUS. Fill our soul only of YOU. Purify our minds, cleanse us too. I want to grab hold of YOUR Holy Robe. Just touches of Heaven, Oh save my soul, Oh save my soul.

Just a touch of Heaven take me Home. I am but a lamb at YOUR feet; Oh at your mercy, I call to YOU my LORD. I take in stride all I can do for you. Purify my human mind. Oh I ask of YOU. I know, I travel not alone, YOU Oh LORD are there, everywhere, I may roam. A glimpse, a touch of Heaven, Oh please, take Oh, take me Home.

I spread YOUR loving name. I, Oh I make YOU known. Help me endure trials, secure me from sharp edged stones that are rapidly thrown. Roses bloom, roses die. A touch of Heaven beyond the sky.

Your Blood

JESUS, YOU gave up YOUR life not just for me, but for all. You could have turned YOUR head, but YOU gave YOUR blood instead. Oh, Oh, Oh YOU gave YOUR blood for us all.

YOU gave YOUR life for all our sins and imperfect ways. We all make our share of mistakes. YOU are so divine, gracious and pure. YOU are everyone's example, our SAVIOR, our cure.

We are to follow YOU each and everyday. For it was YOUR blood, YOUR sacrifice that has shown us the way. Your blood, your tears and despair will never be in vain. For there are some who will never forget YOUR ultimate pain.

Can you see?

Oh can you see? Can you see the twists and turns? Can you
see? Do you yearn? Do you? Would you for evermore?
Would you like to know what's in store? Can you see? Do
you hear? Open your heart, shed those tears.

Can you see clearly now? Do not give up hope to what HE
can do. HE loves, HE can save you. HE knows who you
are, your every care. Can you see? HE'S everywhere.

Can you see? Open your eyes. HIS love for you is magnified.
HE will clear the way. Just call out HIS name. Drop to your
knees. Oh call to HIM and pray.

Can you see? Can it be? Give all to HIM, you will be free.
Let JESUS take your hand. Can you see now? Can you
understand? Can you see? Let JESUS take your hand. Can you
see now? Do you understand?

Always There

I travel within your heart. I'M always there, every place you go. I will never leave you. I'M always there in your soul.

MY love for you will never change. Oh child, you are MINE, I know your pain. I know your name. Can you hear me? MY love for you will never change.

Even though you cannot see ME, I know you can feel me. I am all around, if you want me enough, I can be found.

I will never flee from your soul. Everywhere you turn, no matter where you go I am always there, deep within your soul. Do you feel ME, child? I will never let you go. I am always there, I will always care. I will always be there.

I am everywhere, Oh everywhere.

Everywhere We Are

Hide and seek, you assume it's just a game. The instant you have that sensation, you then realize the chances of hiding from HIM is really mundane.

If you shall seek the Truth of existing pure love. HE'S all around not just above. Hiding is never an option, it just prolongs the inevitable. Keep your eye on the prize, desire the attainable.

HE is all that we need. Everywhere we are. Reachable when falling and there when we grieve. Today we owe HIM, is utterly an understatement. HE brought our sins to erase them again.

Our souls rise, for they were redeemed with a price. Everywhere we are, HE'S already been. HE knows us, inside and out, Oh HE knows our every whim.

Everywhere we go, everywhere we are, we are never alone. Our journey is elsewhere, a place called Home.

Empty Souls

I travel on narrow windy paths on gloomy days and some
nights. I look at this world with many tears and ask myself
what gives anybody the right? The right to disgrace our LORD, to
mock, to disregard HIS existence, HIS glorious ways, HIS
love.

Do you realize all that HE is? HIS residences lies way
beyond any cloud up above. Do you recall what anguishing
measures HE took for you and I?

The fact remains it is written and for us, HE knew HE had to
die. Oh, I want to feel YOUR SPIRIT, Oh LORD. I know that YOU
are real. Oh, I just want more of YOU. I feel, I know there are too
many empty souls. I know empty souls, empty hearts and
empty souls falling apart.

Envy, a little revenge on the run. Fill in all troubles with slugs
from a smoking gun. Logic is out. Man, that ship has sailed.
No! Now you scream and shout, talk about fail. Empty souls
scampering to and fro. Lost without CHRIST. Follow HIS light.
For that is where to go.

Faded Memories

One ragged book, torn apart. Pages scattered near and far. Love and feelings lost beyond a shadow of a doubt. A river with two points corresponding and to YOU, I must bow. Some pages remind me of faded memories. Drifting and just not existing anymore. Oh won't YOU please tell me, tell me, for me what's in store?

I love YOU every day my LORD, more and more. Everyone and anything compared to you are just far and few faded memories. For YOU are my destiny. I am, I remain what YOU want me to be. Give me the right perspective, show me what YOU want me to see. Oh, YOU are more than just faded memories.

I will never forget, Oh never, not me. Forever in YOUR debt, I will always be. Faded memories that's just what they are. But my JESUS, YOU'RE in my soul, I know that I am not alone. Oh LORD, YOU know my fate. Memories will just fade, fade away. YOU will always stay the same. Oh YOU, my LORD never will change. I don't want to be just another faded memory, Oh just another faded memory.

Inner Voice

Tried to hide my face from YOU, knowing full well I never can flee from the Truth. Many times I have ignored that inner voice, bluntly and boldly pointing out to me to make the right choice. Connecting desires one by one. A failure to respond to that inner voice. Now it's practically gone.

There are days I want to hide and run away. There are other days where I am not so ashamed. Where I look to HIM for knowledge, kneel down and pray.

An inner voice is deep within us, all day and night. To look is to know. To shun HIM is a frightful feeling. To reach out for HIM is a new beginning. Guidance is always approaching our hearts ever so slightly. HE speaks to all souls. Just listen to HIS soothing voice, HE then will lead you to a place of rejoice.

In us we all have that inner voice. You can try to be untruthful to yourself; journey to a hole of pity and self-doubt. Listen to JESUS, your inner voice; you then will void out the skepticism and embark on the embracing route.

So let your inner voice speak loud and true, JESUS is trying to get through. We all have an inner voice. Just know that JESUS speaks to you.

Let Our Children Pray

It would be a great triumph in time, OH on that miraculous
day. Oh let us lead the way. Let our children pray. Society
took praying out of schools. Wow, what's next? How cruel!
Oh the world would be in such a peaceful state, if we banish
all this hate. Oh please on this day; finally we
let our children pray.

Come out and help display. Oh let our children pray.

Pray in the morning, noon, and night. Pray in their schools.
Oh what a sight! Pray for every thought on their mind. Let
our children pray. GOD will listen. HE has the time. Let our
children pray. Please do not take that
away; Oh that away.

What Are We?

I will praise YOU. I will pray to YOU JESUS. I will raise my
hands in YOUR Honor. I will pray in YOUR Glory. Where have we
gone to? Where has our Faith faded to? Where are we?
Who are we now? Oh JESUS help us be found.

Too many lost. Where are we now? Self-satisfaction and
results in all life's distraction. YOU are my hope. YOU are my
will. I will pray in YOUR glory.

Where have we gone to? Where has our Faith faded to?
Where are we? Who are we now? Oh JESUS help
us be found.

Too many lost. Where are we? Where are we now? The
world consumes and swallows whole. Let the Angels assist
and reveal, reveal who YOU are and what YOU'VE done, and
not a fable but reality. I will pray in YOUR Glory.

Where are we? Take away this apathy and let us soak in
YOUR Glory. Are we numb? What have we become?

After All

I look back from time to time on an inkling of my life. YOU could never forget; but we must forever forgive. If you have the faith and trust in HIM all the way. After all, shall we not listen to everything our LORD JESUS has to convey?

After all look and feel all that HE did for all that HE loves. After all HE lives in Heaven above. Think positive. Is the glass half empty? Or is it really half full? You make the call. I believe our heart is our main tool. After all JESUS, we are to strive to be like YOU.

Oh LORD, lead us to that goal we must pursue. Take us after all with YOU, Oh with YOU.

Grow With JESUS

It seems to me like a glimpse of fiction and non-reality. I want to know, Oh how I want to grow. I want JESUS in my heart, I want HIM deep within my soul. HE is a way, our only way. A glimpse of fiction and non-reality, HE indeed died for us. Oh our SALVATION, our CAVALRY.

I want to grow with JESUS, my hand in HIS hand. I want to follow all the way; I wish to understand. It is reality. I know that others take it for granted. Everything HE did for everybody. I want to grow with; Oh, I want to grow with my SAVIOR everyday, never to cease. Put my hand in HIS hand. Let my love for HIM increase.

JESUS, JESUS my reality. My life has felt like fiction, but YOU are real to me. There are people that do not believe, that deny YOU. Maybe it's possible that they are unable to see. It's more than a glimpse, like a stone between the eyes.

I want to grow with JESUS. HE is our reality. HE is not fiction. JESUS is as real as you and me. I want to grow with JESUS. Oh JESUS, will you set me free, me free, Oh me free?

Run Free

It is simply just an awesome feeling with JESUS by my side. Guiding me day and night, knowing that I will be lead by HIS Holy Light. I know that one glorious day or night my soul will take flight. All will be worth it without a doubt. My soul will run free.

Just that thought alone, look what my LORD JESUS did for me. A slave no more will I be, for my soul will run free. Through HIS love, blood and mercy I shout to THEE. Thank You SAVIOR! YOU set me free. No ill thought will be in the air, Just my soul running free. Halleluiah no despair. Thank You my MAJESTY now my soul can finally run free.

Another Life

My friend I see the mess you're in. Don't close your heart right now. All you are to be is not a misconception. Open your eyes and you shall capture and behold another life.

Another life so different than before. Once you include the LORD, your heart will be whole again. Another life begins after the storm. All is possible; nothing is in vain without knowing JESUS and what HE can do.

Another life, another skin that's what HE can give you. My friend I see the mess you're in. HE'S just asking for your confession. All you are to be is not a misconception.

If another life is what you desire beg for HIS mercy. HE already forgives and in us all HE forever lives.

Do You Know?

Do you know where Heaven is? Would you come with me?
Would you want to take that journey? Do you want to see?
Do you trust in our LORD, Our KING?

Let's go tell all, let's shout and sing. Do you feel the way
I do right now today? Do you want to go to Heaven? JESUS
knows the way.

Do you feel HIM deep within your heart and soul? Let's get
ready. It's almost time to go. Can you feel HIS tender
caress all over you? Dear friend, do you even know what HE
went through? Do you know where Heaven is? Would you
like to see all burdens cast away and our souls set free?

I Want to Walk with You

LORD Oh my SAVIOR, my merciful KING. You mean everything, everything to me. I want YOU and need YOU everyday. These words I say. These words I pray. Anything YOU ask me to I will do. Oh my precious JESUS, I want to walk with YOU.

YOU'RE my glowing light. Oh I want to hold YOU tight. My trials and errors, YOU will get me through. Oh I want to follow, I want to walk with YOU. I think of YOU each and everyday. These words I say. These words I pray.

In my heart and in my soul, I know I trust in YOU. YOU are my only ONE. I want to walk with YOU. I know what YOU did for me, I can never repay. These words I say, these words I pray. I know down deep inside I trust in YOU.

Oh my precious SAVIOR, I'm ready. I want to walk with YOU. I love YOU. YOU are only what is true. I want to walk with YOU.

Glorify

I do speak of YOU. I do sing of YOU. Oh and I praise, I glorify YOUR name, since I found YOU. I have and never will feel the same.

I specify YOUR great precious name. Some will never receive YOU. YOUR grace in their soul. My heart just shatters knowing that entering heaven wasn't their goal.

To love YOU, Oh LORD, is to glorify YOUR precious name. As long, until the day I die, even after, YOUR name I will glorify.

The fire inside, all my devotion to YOU I cannot hide. Oh YOUR name, Dear JESUS, I will glorify.

One More Prayer

Tell me of this world, what I have to offer YOU. Anything I have for YOU seems so microscopic, or anything I do. I do however obtain a soul and I owe it all to YOU.

The more I think about YOU, how YOU walked among men, saved souls from sin. When I feel so misled by the devious world and polluted air, I cry Dear JESUS, Oh please hear one, one more prayer. For it is all I give to YOU, my soul is already YOURS.

When I feel like I'm about to break I say one more prayer to remedy the ache. If YOU I couldn't reach, Oh what would I do?

One more plea, one more confession, YOU and only YOU are my obsession.

So I say to YOU, one more prayer to get me through. One more prayer to YOU.

Stones

Everyone from time to time can relate to this notion. JESUS certainly did all the time, HE walked among men. Even though all He wanted to do is rid this sad world of sin. Throw one stone collect them all. Throw another, watch them fall. Ever feel this way at all?

Too many stones cast out from you, left to right. Do you endure the pain? Stay with HIM and fight. Or do you drop your jaw and flee in vain? Oh do you get taken over with fright? Tell me, Oh tell me, cast stones all around me. I know I will not fail. Oh GOD willing I will prevail. You who hide beneath the fire, my flesh is of YOU, but my soul will soar higher.

David used a stone to drop his foe. Tell me friend, which stone are you apt to throw? Stones for the good or stones for the bad? I have JESUS, so throw all you have. Throw one stone collect them all. Throw another, watch them fall. Everyone from time to time can relate to this notion. Some stones should remain in the ocean.

Anymore

I belong to YOU, Oh my LORD. All of me, every bit, take it all.
Often I say take it and all of my humanity. Don't need it,
not anymore. All this world brings, it takes more. So I just
don't need this world, this world I can do without.

A second away from YOU, I'd rather not think that way. I just
have no use, Oh for this world anymore, since I have YOU in
my life, in my soul. I don't need anymore.

Some may say they can do anything by themselves and
I say without YOU, we will ultimately plunge to failure.
Without YOU anything we attempt will be engulfed by
doom. No matter what, everything we pursue since I have
YOU in my life, and I feel YOU inside my soul, I say this now
if without YOU, what's living for? I need YOU. I don't need
this world anymore, anymore, anymore.

I Remember When

Reminiscing and missing, that's what I do. I can't and
won't ever forget you. You will always be a huge part of
my heart. Remember 'til death do us part. Even that being
true, still there's a piece of me missing in the dark.

I remember when I would bring you to a smile. Oh and
I remember when we would have discussions about the
bible. You had such a glow about you. You simply lit up
every room you walked into. It is not easy at all to make a
brand new start. One thing I feel and know you will forever
be kept in my heart.

I remember when I would see you, your spirit two clouds above
seven. Now look at you someday entering Heaven.
I just want to say that we will be joined together someday.
Just ponder this, for you no more suffering or sickness.
You received your ticket to the Pearly Gates. GOD willing as
awesome as HE is. I will be there as well and my face you'll see. We
will bow to JESUS, our MAJESTY.

I remember when, every memory.

Every Knee Will Bow

It is time to confront all your demons and step over here.
This is the place, a place to overcome all fears. There's
a place and time for everything. It is only your choice
to make. Be very certain cuz it's all at stake. My place
of redemption, salvation and the purest love. Have you
guessed? It's my SAVIOR who resides above.

There's no time like now. If you believe then you know
every knee will bow. There's so much to address. Oh yeah
every tongue will confess. To some, what an unfathomable
concept. Swallow it cuz it's the truth. No one's immune.

Everyone will witness and choices will be obsolete. You
had your chance to simply believe in our KING.

There will come a day, maybe soon every knee will bow;
that includes you. You have that choice now.

What in Heaven's name are you going to do?

There You Are

Even if one is blind they know that YOU are not far. Let's
face it everywhere we look, it's amazing, there YOU are.
Never doubt about how and what YOU can do. Let's face it
every awesome occasion, well it's all because of YOU.

Everywhere I turn, even when I crash and burn It's safe
to say that you're not far. My beloved JESUS, there you are,
There you are, there you are.

It blows me away that no matter what we do or say, YOU
forgive and in our hearts you remain. There YOU are, there YOU
are. Through thick and thin let's face it, YOU gave all
for our sins.

Can't ever Thank You enough Dear JESUS for all that YOU do.
I Know it's only all because of YOU.

All It Takes

Do you know of all love? Do you know HIS face? Can you
feel HIS pain? Oh everything HE longs to embrace? The HOLY
ONE, who cured all ailments, including chasing out sin. Have
you now heard of HIM? Do you do everything you can?

Do you know my JESUS? Do you know this man? You do
not have to be in such dire straights. I know a man,
that's all it takes. Would you collect all HIS tears up
on that cross? Would you suffer as HE and set all free? You
do not have to wait. Put down that fragment of
distrust, no time to hesitate. I know a man.
HE is all it takes.

Last Breath

Think forward, not back. Throw caution to the wind,
take Faith with no slack. Don't you give in; take a little
time. Love in CHRIST, we all must find. Don't you give in to
all this world's demise. For all we need is JESUS CHRIST.

How do you feel now? This could be your last breath.
Contemplate, swallow it and bow. JESUS did and gave all
still to this day. We owe HIM everything, whatever it takes.

HE, our SAVIOR took HIS last breath, up on that cross. HE took
and carried our sin for a cost. We ought to be very grateful
for all that we have. Take a deep breath it could be your
last. Life is too short. Days fly by fast. So hold on to JESUS
and never look back.

Do not wallow. Do not fret. You never know it just might be
your last breath. Pray and know in your heart that your last
breath can be a brand new start. Relinquish all of your fears
and regrets. For it could be your very last breath.

Throw caution to the wind and take Faith with no slack.
Take a deep
breath, it could be your last.

The Miracle of Life

From the shelter, from the manger, from day one, YOU
JESUS, knew that YOU would face and endure every ounce of
danger. Oh my LORD, Oh my SAVIOR, only YOU, YOUR blood,
YOUR life has released me. Take my soul, Oh please make me
whole. I shall follow YOU in day, I will follow YOU at
night. YOU'RE my reason, Oh the miracle of life.

Shine YOUR light for me. Thank You JESUS for all YOUR love
and mercy. Let me bathe in YOUR love, Oh let me Thank
all the Angels above. YOU'RE all that I strive for. YOU'RE
the miracle of life. For me my LORD, YOU died for. Forgive
them FATHER, for they know not what they have done.

True and merciful words spoken out of the mouth of GOD'S
only SON. For everyone YOU died. Oh JESUS, YOU are the
miracle of life.
YOU are the pentacle. YOU are the miracle of life. Thank You
Oh my JESUS for all that YOU do.

We All Need

Sometimes, some days we all need a little more. Some days
we all question, wonder what's in store. You can try to deny
it. Sometimes we just need more. More Love, more Strength,
more Love, more Faith. We all need more o any given day.
We all need JESUS to clear the way.

You can try to conceal it, never want to reveal it. Or you can
accept it or admit it. We all need HIM more and more.
HE holds our future, our dreams, forevermore. We all need to have a
lot more. More knowledge about HIM, to end the war.

We all need HIM the most from the highest mountain, to coast
to coast, to reach the depths of Heaven only through HIM. I'm
speaking of the HOLY GHOST. The love of JESUS, we need
fulfilled day and night. HE is the way, Oh HE restores life.

We need more Love, more Strength, more Hope, more
Faith. We all need more on any given day. We all need JESUS
to clear the way. We need HIM. We need HIM so. To find HIM,
is to not let HIM go.

A Gift

Something so memorable such as a kiss or a hug. Hold
on to the memory, for it is a gift of love, from the Heavens
above. There are so many virtues in life, the good, the
bad. It is said all of us each have a gift, if we seek we
shall find. Get up, get moving it is not possible
to freeze time.

A gift from our GOD should be used and shared everyday.
Each and everyone have a gift. If it is not used it will soon
vanish away. A gift from Heaven, so do not save it for
a rainy day.

If you know your true calling I urge you to use it. Share
it every day. A true heart is a gift, a soul for CHRIST. Well
that's why we exist. We must utilize our gift after they are
received everyday and every night. For no one can destroy
the bond, our chemistry we have with CHRIST.

A gift from GOD is so surreal to receive. It's our job to do
GOD'S work. It is everything we must achieve. A gift from
Heaven is more than remarkable. This, Oh this
you must believe.

It Is Said

It is said that GOD so loved the world, HE gave HIS only
BEGOTTEN SON. It is said Thy will, will be done. If that's the
case why is there so many selfish and evil hearts? We all
need to rebuke Satan to turn our lives around, make
more than just a brand new start.

It is said that JESUS is the way, HE is the light. It is said,
it is written from beginning to the end all the tools and
knowledge well, it is written for all of us to see. Oh for all
of us to read. JESUS walked the earth a long, long time ago.
Turning no one away Helping and doing everything HE
could. GOD had a plan, if we can do anything to help, I think
we should.

It is said that JESUS is the way, the light. We all need to
merge together, love one another and praise HIS great name.
It is said that GOD so loved the world, HE gave HIS only
BEGOTTEN SON. Can you say the same?

Think about CHRIST. HE does live in you and me. Now it's
up to the world to finally see.

Without Jesus

A ripple in the ocean, waves come crashing through. Think
about it, we are like the ocean, all we need to calm the
waves is YOU. Oh JESUS, YOU are the ONE. Without YOU, we're
scattered souls on the run. Oh Heaven, if YOU can hear me,
throw down a sign. And if YOU feel me, drop me down a
line. Lift me up, out of this raging sea. And if YOU can, will
YOU please set my soul free?

YOU know me, YOU know me well. Without JESUS, all I
would and all I could is fail. Catch me if I happen to fall.
Without JESUS, who would hear my call? I know JESUS,
without YOU, my life would be on pause. Without JESUS there
wouldn't be a cause.

With YOUR blood, YOUR life, YOU have paved the way. So in
honor to YOU, I will open my heart and pray.

A ripple in the ocean, waves come crashing through. Oh,
without YOU JESUS, what could I do?
What, oh what, could I do?

Choices

We all have choices we need to make. Take the right steps
for goodness sake. The choices we select, the paths we
embark on, all the same tune yet a different song. YOU, Oh
LORD, have given us chance after chance. If we stare long
enough, well look at that, glance after glance. The choices
we make in our life, time after time. Is it really
enough for all that we strive?

All the love in this world, Oh why does it hide? JESUS, Dear
LORD, please show us the way. Help us to fight, help us.
Prepare us for that day. Good must overcome evil. Well
that's what I say. We all are in this specific place for a
reason. I feel if we disregard the LORD, well that's treason.
Each and every one of us have choices to make.

If we are to follow in JESUS' footsteps, our greatest Example,
the Purest Light, we must partake. For if we do not, our souls
are at stake. We all have choices we need to make. Let's
follow JESUS for goodness sake.
Oh for goodness sake.

Heal Me Tonight

Sometimes I lose my way, Oh LORD. You know that sometimes
I go astray. Show me, tell me that it will be alright.
Oh JESUS, heal me tonight. Yeah, yeah just hold me tight.
Show me YOUR light. Heal me tonight. JESUS show me all of
YOUR ways. Teach me every blessed day.

JESUS teach me, hold me, shed light on YOUR mercy. Turn
dark into light; Oh heal me tonight. YOUR tears, YOUR despair,
YOUR blood. In return YOUR love hovers everywhere. YOU, Oh
JESUS, are my answer. YOU are not a mystery. YOU'RE face to
face. Someday I surely will see. Life can plummet; spirits
may rise. Hold me tight, Oh BELOVED Heal me,
yes, Heal me tonight.

I trust YOU in every way. Teach me all of YOUR love. You can
look into my eyes, tell that everything, everything will be all
right. Embrace, YOUR arms around me, heal me tonight.
Oh, my Gracious LORD, heal me, heal me tonight. I trust in
YOU all the way. Heal me tonight or today. Just heal me in
every way. Heal me. Hear my plea. Heal me, set me free.

Show me YOUR light. Heal, just heal me
tonight, tonight, tonight.

I Hold On To You

It is astonishing to say the least, what YOU do and mean to me. It's amazing when I hold on to YOU I know, I know I'm free. I know YOU exist. I will do anything; pursue everything, whatever the risk. I hold onto YOU. YOU'RE
forever, forever true.

Thank You, Oh JESUS, Thank YOU for all that YOU are. All the love that YOU show, I hold on to YOU as tight as I can. Never, Oh never, to let YOU go.

YOU are so forever, forever all I need. It's safe to say
YOU know my heart. My soul YOU can see.
I hold on to all of YOU. Do not let me go. I hold, I hold on.
YOUR love is all I know.

My Promise

I say unto you, I say to thee, you must obey and worship ME. I created everything living that you see. I can make anything come to an end, only ME. Live for ME and ME only. I created you. I created life. Trust in ME, I will lead you to victory.

My promise to you: I will give you Eternal Life. Obey MY word for I am day. I am night. I promise you a place in Heaven. Where there is neither death nor sorrow. To you, I cannot promise you tomorrow. My SON JESUS walked the earth, shed HIS blood for MY word. He died for you, up on the cross. He took your Sins for a cost. Only through HIM you shall receive a place in Heaven and Victory.

I love the world, I gave it life. The only way to Eternal Life is through my SON JESUS CHRIST. Spread MY Love to every soul. Reach out to others you reap what you sow.

Book Of Life

Flood my soul with all YOUR love. Instill in me from Heaven
above. Teach me what my FATHER expects. Teach me of
purest Love, erase all regrets. I want to see YOU, FATHER. I
want to hear YOUR voice. I want to fly to Heaven. I want to
rejoice. I want to forever remain in the book of life. I want
to see YOUR nail scarred hands. Oh my, Wonderful
JESUS CHRIST.

I pray to THEE, I feel, I am not worthy. For all that YOU
did, for all that YOU are. YOU are simply amazing, all
this world offers YOU are scars. Love, Faith and Hope for YOU
are all I have. I know YOU are all that I need. Only YOU can
wipe all my sins clean.

I cry when, oh I cry when I think about YOU, everyday
through and through.

The Writing On The Wall

Words set in stone once were shattered by a man in pure
rage; so back to the mountain, back to the first stage. The
SHEPARD came down again with words set in stone. He was
a leader of GOD'S army. He encountered a burning bush; he
finally believed. He knew right then and there GOD sought
him out. All of his people he must lead.

Even when Moses was instructed by our FATHER to dip his
staff into the water so they wouldn't die, they still were
not believers. But the writing on the wall too blind to see,
too dense to feel; Faith was too small, too blind to see the
writing on the wall.

Hope for many were lost. They were slain, they had to fall.
They failed to see the writing on the wall. We must hang on
to Faith and see the writing on the wall.

Right By My Side

JESUS, YOU are Almighty. YOU always seem to be watching over everybody. I owe YOU my heart. I owe YOU my soul. I know it's not enough so the story goes. YOUR story will live on and never die. YOU are so much alive and right by my side.

Whenever I feel like I'm sinking in the quick sand of life. That's when YOU fill my soul and tell me that everything will be all right. YOU are right by my side. YOU are with me when my heart and world collide.

I know I can trust YOU. I know YOU are alive. YOU won't deceive me, YOU'RE right by my side. Oh YOU will never leave me, this I know. LORD, I will follow YOU wherever YOU go. I am human, just a man. YOU love me anyway just the way that I am.

YOU are my LEADER, I love and trust everyday. Oh JESUS, yes right by my side, I know YOU will stay. YOU and only YOU can deliver our souls to our FATHER up above. Oh JESUS will YOU please show this world about YOUR love? YOU have died on that cross. Oh my LORD, YOU were crucified. YOU rose from the dead to be right by my side, right by my side. Oh my LORD, YOU are right by my side, right by my side. I know YOU are alive, I can feel YOU right by my side.

No Longer Lost

Seek and refuge or just a way out, but I was blind. Always stumbling in the dark, no landmarks I find. I was too blind to see all the wrong places at all the wrong times. I know now that I can't rewind my life. I needed something, the right way out. I cried for an answer so full of doubt. I felt different, like brand-new. I heard YOUR voice, it can only be YOU. I knew I was no longer lost, just follow YOUR voice. Trust in YOU, for YOU are the right choice.

Know that YOU and only YOU are the way. If ever you feel lost, hope right down the drain. Humble yourself, open your heart. Call out HIS name. JESUS feels your every pain. He will wipe your eyes and stop the rain. You will find your way just listen to what your heart has to say. Grab hold of Our SAVIOR'S hand, clasp onto it as tight as you can. Life can wash away like a grain of sand.

HE loves all of us the same. JESUS will pull you from the darkness. HE will stop the rain. HE has calmed many Storms. HE has hushed raging seas. There is nothing on this earth that HE would not do for you and me. No longer lost, you can feel HIM all around. No longer lost but now are found. You are now found. Whatever the cost you are no longer lost.

I Will Stand My Ground

Help him don't push him down. He's just standing his
ground. Please do not mock or stab him in the back. It is only
knowledge of CHRIST you lack. Just believe that JESUS loves all
of us more than life itself. So put your money away it's not
about wealth. I will not let you back this follower down. I
have no problem standing my ground. I stand my ground. I stand
proudly, heart and soul. No matter what I never will let
go.

I have all my Hope, Faith in my LORD. So please step down. I
will hold, I will stand my ground. No matter what wall you
seem to construct around you, it's apparent that CHRIST can
always break through. Help anyone in need. Think twice next
time you want to see or make someone else bleed.
Know that CHRIST died up on that cross blood, tears and love.

HE gave up HIS life for our FATHER up above. It was HIS will. It
was HIS deed. For our sins HE had to bleed. HE had to die for
everyone, HE is our example, HE is a perfect SON. I will not
back down. I am here to stand my ground, stand my ground,
and stand my ground.

In My Heart

I know that I can't always figure out or understand why.
Why murderers sometimes slip through the system. Then
we have to see our young children die. They say that there
is good in every one of us. If that is true why, oh why do we
live in a world of malice and disgust?

In my heart, FATHER deep inside, even though I do not always
concur, I know that you are right. In my heart close to YOU,
YOU'RE always there to ease me through. YOU let Angels save
lives everyday. Thank YOU GOD for sending Angels our way.
Wings or not I will fly away. In my heart YOU always have a
place. I know I do not always see YOUR reasons or
comprehend YOUR master plan. Maybe someday I will finally
grasp it, even understand. In my heart it tears me up inside
to see the world annihilate itself right in front of me.

In my heart, in my soul, Oh GOD there's so many answers
to questions I want to know. In my heart YOU are the air I
breathe. In my soul YOU are all that I need.

I Will For You

Here I am, here I stay. Sometimes just clenching my throat LORD, grasping for a word or two just to say. I know I have some work to do. I know I have people to seek. It's all about YOU. YOU, oh Dear LORD, that's why I'm here. YOU, oh Dear LORD, that's why I'm here to tell whoever I can without a morsel of fear. I will for YOU do everything YOU ask of me. I will for YOU LORD, gladly open my eyes to finally see. What YOU willingly did for the world for it is undeniably reality.

Oh LORD how can my life be as YOURS? I owe YOU everything, my MERCIFUL LORD. Take it, take all that I give. I Thank You. It is because of YOU that I live. I will for YOU, speak the truth. Open my mouth and utter words only for YOU. Come down take me now. I am waiting for that day. I will for YOU, now stay and pray.

I will for YOU, spread YOUR love where I am. YOU are so very gracious I wait for you. I will for YOU, make a stand. I will for YOU, stand on the highest mountain, dig the deepest hole. I will for YOU, willingly give YOU my soul.

Go With Hope

I see you everyday, I hear what you say. I love you in every
way. You may not see or understand everything. There is a
plan. Some things are not meant to be seen. I see, I feel, I
know. Come child, go with hope. Stand up, do not run. Do
not hide. Remember for you, I laid down my life. I bought
you with MY blood for a price. Follow ME, for
I am JESUS CHRIST.

I love you in every way, I hear child what you say. Go with
hope, go today. I am truly the SON of GOD. I am truly the
only way. Follow ME, there is no time to waste. Put all your
Faith in ME. Open your heart, I will set you free.

Go with hope, Go with love. Shine your light for Heaven
above. Share with all the love inside, for it was not in vain
that I died. I say to you, listen clear. Go with hope child, I
feel your tears.

Go with hope, go with faith, go tell all face to face. I am
coming back. I will return again. All that do follow, I will
surely win. The trumpet will sound, all will hear on judgment
day. Some will fear. Go with hope. Tell of me. Go
with hope I will set you free. Child be free.

One Question

When I limp down the bizarre and deserted pathway. When I swallow and think back to the past was there another way? Or another day and so much dismay. As I travel, as I leap to that time, as I stumble, as I crash. After all it's my dime. Oh are YOU there? If YOU are do YOU even care? Oh I've got one question are YOU even there? Can YOU answer me? Can YOU set me free? I need YOU not later but now. I need, oh I need you LORD. Restore me somehow.

Are YOU there? Well are YOU? Show me, show me YOU care. Life isn't always great. Sometimes it isn't always fair. Oh are YOU there? If YOU are, do YOU even care? Oh I've got one question are YOU even there? Do YOU even care?

LORD listen, hear me clear. All I have right now are these tears. When I look back I see fallen years. This is a different time a different day. I have given my heart to JESUS. HE has shown me the way.

Guide Me Through

LORD take my life and lead me through. YOU have all
control, oh please guide me through. I am but a man. Sin
free I'm not. I can say though dear JESUS you're all I've got
in this life or whatever it may be YOU will always remain
my SAVIOR my CAVALRY.

I just want to shed light of YOU for more than just a few. I
can't do it on my own I need YOU to guide me through. Any
gift I receive from above I will not waste it and I will share
to any with pure love.

I know I am of skin. I also know that this is not the end.
Any pain in my head limited to just lie in bed. I know I can
count on YOU. Oh for YOU'RE the only one that can and will
guide me through. Oh YOU'RE the only
one to guide me through.

Give or Take

Take a chance, walk that line. Put someone before yourself.
Ah, perhaps another time. I step out of darkness, I am now
drawn to the light. I travel to the ONE who holds the light. It
is, it is the only way.

Give or take, would you rather give everything you won or
take everything and be completely alone? What a fatal
mistake. Give or take away, do you continue to want a whole
lot more of this world?

This frivolous place, it really isn't ours to take. Would you
give everything you own to one day be with the MAN, the
MAN who saved your soul? Isn't that more than enough to
give everything that you own?

Give or take, would you rather give from your heart
everything you own or take everything selfishly? Would you
rather lose your soul with your darkened ways and be
completely alone? Give or take, the answer is your own.

Take A Look

HOLY FATHER, oh your MAJESTY. I take a long hard look at this
world and this is what I see:

I see people on the streets not knowing who YOU are. I see
misers taking everything way too far. Oh how far we've
come, how far we've strayed. We must not take for granted
the price YOU paid.

Just watching the news day in and day out. Knowing and
hearing all the despicable evil in this world, kind of makes
one doubt. Doubt and wonder how cruel and corrupted
people can be. If they just opened the BIBLE well it would be
one step closer to victory.

We all need to just take a look, a look deep within our
hearts. We all need to drop and pray to make
a brand new start.

I Want To Go

All that I desire is YOU, oh LORD. All that I long for, oh Is for
that glorious day. All I want to do is go with YOU. Waiting
for that time, oh waiting for that day. These are my wishes
I want to convey.

When you come back, oh JESUS CHRIST, I want to know when
YOU fly back to Heaven can I go? I want to go, I want to go
to be with YOU. Oh JESUS that is the only thing I want to do.
I want to go with YOU.

Oh yeah, oh HEAVENLY FATHER when YOU come back to claim
all of YOUR believers and turn away all of the deceivers.
Oh LORD, on that glorious day; and now I stay, just waiting,
waiting for that day.

Open Up

Open up, don't shut down. Grab a hand, gather around.
JESUS I'm falling, can YOU catch me? JESUS I'm calling, can
YOU hear me?

Oh I love you LORD that is true, oh JESUS. I know that
nothing is possible. Oh nothing is possible without the
grace of YOU!

Oh I often open up, open up to YOU. Let's all open up. Let's
all be true. Let's all be honest to YOU! If we were to speak
our mind and still be kind, open up and let YOU in.

Open up, open up, let YOU in. Then I say we must begin.
Open up I say. Oh please will YOU stay? Oh please let us
Open up and not shut down. Open up to each other and stop
messing around.

I Can See

In all that we do, sometimes we forget. Forget what is true
and that is YOU. Oh LORD, our JESUS, I fear not YOUR name. I
will shout it aloud every passing day.

Oh, oh, oh, ah, eh. I bow down to YOU, oh LORD. Ah, ah,
ah. Oh I can see, I can see the world all around. Oh and
I can see, I can see from the mountain tops to the ground.
I proudly say that you are my KING, for that I will
graciously sing!

Oh I say you are KING. Oh LORD to all YOU are, our everything,
our wonderful king! Oh, oh, oh, eh, eh, eh. So I say
unto YOU and now I bow. I can see, I can see clearly now!

The Cross

It's no secret the suffering and agony that did certainly take place. Oh the price YOU paid for the torturer and us; oh I cannot even fathom the pain. The look of torment on YOUR forgiving face.

YOU carried the cross with blood, love and forgiveness. With Salvation, Redemption and Pure Pride. We all need to remember, we'll keep in mind not only how YOU lived, but also how YOU died.

Through all YOUR demise and YOUR will, healing us we do feel. Oh the cross, the cross that saved each and every one of us. YOU, our SAVIOR, JESUS CHRIST. YOU, HIS only SON.

Have I Told You

Have I told YOU that I love and appreciate YOU, well I do.
Oh and have I said to YOU that one day and only one-way
that I want to see YOU? Oh I only hope that there are many
and not just a few to be in YOUR open arms
and to be with YOU.

YOU are our MASTER, our CREATOR the only ONE. I can't say
enough; YOU gave up for us YOUR only SON. And for that our
work for YOU is never done. Have I told YOU that YOU'RE
an awesome GOD and ever so forgiving? And for that I'm
living, living for YOU. But do not forget I only work for YOU.
Well I do.

Let's get to work. Our job is incomplete. We long for the
day that we will meet.

Tears On My Pillow

Tears on my pillow, thinking of you. Can't seem to grasp anything else. I miss you so very much. I miss your voice, smile and touch. I won't ever forget you, nor the time we shared together. I will always love you, forever and ever. There's no cure for the way that I feel. Nothing for the numbness, no remedy that will heal, that will heal my scarred heart. I just never pictured us so far apart.

I pray everyday and every night for a chance just to hold you tight. I feel so empty, I feel so crushed. I miss your love but I know one day we'll meet above. Oh yeah, oh yeah.

Our love can never be forgotten you're always on my mind. I try my best but it seems that it is never right. I live one day at a time. My mind is always on the go, I wish I could have told you goodbye and you knew I was holding your hand, right there by your side. I will think of you, oh every day. I hope you're listening to what I have to say.

Love you, miss you, see you.

You Chose Me

YOU chose me, long before I really knew YOU. At that time YOUR life was at stake. YOU chose me, now I choose YOU. And in YOU, LORD my heart throttles with Faith.

YOU knew me way before I even knew myself. On the cross YOU died. YOU knew me even before I was alive. YOU chose me then, so now I choose YOU. YOU loved me and now I profess my love to YOU.

YOU know my life, YOU know me inside and out. For YOU I will bow. YOU chose me, so I choose YOU now. Oh JESUS, I choose YOU now.

YOU chose me, YOU loved me, YOU are my destiny. I am in debt to YOU, my MAJESTY. YOU love, YOU chose me, YOU my JESUS first chose me.

Question and Answer

We often wonder what is our purpose here? What do we do now? We do not have all the answers, we do not always know how. It is up to us to find the gifts GOD let us have to share with others and help when we can. We all have questions and not enough answers. We all question why? How can this be? Why did this happen, happen to me?

When we get to Heaven, our blinders will be off and we will finally see. Oh we will all be woken up from this earthly dream. Oh, oh can't you see? Hey this is much bigger than you and me. And together we will finally see.

I know that I have my share of questions. Like why do innocent children die? Oh please tell me why? Why do loved ones leave us? And why do malicious ones get to stay? Oh please tell me, show me your way. Help me comprehend reasons for these harsh but true questions.
Answer we know not. Questions we ask a lot.

Let's Get Together

Hey, hey throw down your sword, your sword of deception.
Get rid, get rid of your hate now. It is time to gather around.
Hold our hands high and bow. Oh yes, bow to our LORD, our
MASTER at hand. Let's all get together and make our stand.

Hey let's get together and praise HIS great name. Let's get
together. We'll never be the same. Come on sisters and
brothers let's shout and sing. For HE is everything, our
loving KING. So let us shout and glorify HIS precious name.

Let us come together. We'll never be the same.

Holy

Why must you find it completely convenient not to believe in HIM? Do you actually think that you're not guilty of committing a single sin? HE is MASTER to everyone and JESUS CHRIST is HIS only BEGOTTEN SON.

Don't take it from me there is a book that is Holy. It will hit you right between the eyes with reality. It is true to say wake up. Flesh will only lead you away. You can't count on your skin and bones. Put your Faith in HIM alone.

GOD created every living thing that exists. Wow all that love, how can you willingly resist? No one's perfect nor free of sin. The Devil is working overtime to pull you in.

No matter where you are, no matter what you do, just remember, GOD had a SON, JESUS died, died for you.

Is it convenient now? Am I getting through?

There Is A Place

There is a place, high above the clouds, where you hear only peaceful sounds. There is a place I know of that is filled with Faith and Pure Love. There is a place, I know of where streets are of gold. There is a book, I know of where words of wisdom are foretold.

No death shall we find. No despair to clutter our minds. There is a place, I know of that is filled with faith and only pure love. I want to see, oh I want to be in that glorious place. That place where the Angels forever sing. I want to sing with the Angels. Raise my voice up high ever to rejoice. Forever to remain with HIM, oh my SAVIOR, for eternal, for eternal life. Someday I will be in that place. I will never quit, never quit the race. There is a place.

What About JESUS?

Are you in a slumber? Are you in a rut? That almost seems impossible to emerge from? Well you may not get it, let alone believe it, but it's true, there are others worse off than you.

There is a MAN, who took the wrath for your blood, oh your soul. Pick, pick up the BIBLE, and onward go.

And just remember you reap, oh you reap what you sow. It's all about choice and reasons. So think next time: what about JESUS?

HE'S the reason you exist. HE'S our love. What about JESUS? HE died for you. That being said, how can you resist? Do you put others before yourself? Open your heart to someone else?

Ask yourself and only you: what about JESUS? For HIM what would you do? Put everything else aside? There's nothing to prove. Just a question for HIM, what do You do? Are you in a slumber? Are you being consumed by the dark and not the light? What about JESUS?

Stand and erase all the sin.

Your Mercy is Your Grace

I have nothing, nothing without YOU. YOUR love is what I thrive on. Oh LORD, YOUR grace, I grasp onto YOUR mercy, your mercy.

Without YOUR mercy there wouldn't be anything, anything that I can do. I want to see YOU face to face. YOU are amazing. YOUR mercy is YOUR grace.

YOU enhance all highs. YOU keep all steadfast at low times. There is no pedestal, we are all the same. In YOUR eyes there is no one or none to blame. I am, we are useless without YOU.

I want to see YOU face to face. YOU are so amazing. YOUR mercy is YOUR grace, YOUR mercy. JESUS, my LORD, your love; you see every flaw and every helping hand.

YOUR mercy is YOUR grace, YOUR mercy is YOUR grace. YOU'RE amazing, so pure, so amazing. YOUR mercy is YOUR grace. I want to be with YOU in that Place.

I Call You SAVIOR

Some refer to YOU in many different ways. I love YOU for saving me on that stormy day. What YOU endured, no one else would and couldn't do. Despite our sins and what we go through Halleluiah, Halleluiah, JESUS YOU willingly gave up your life.

It's all because of YOU, I call YOU SAVIOR, LORD of all KINGS. YOUR mercy, YOUR love, YOUR blood for everyone. Oh how YOU have redeemed. YOU restore our faith when we question why. YOU are there to wipe our tears when we cry. YOU spread words of love when YOU walked among men. YOU knew right then and there that you would die for our sins.

YOU have many awesome names for which YOU stand for. I call YOU, I call YOU my SAVIOR, my SAVIOR.

My King

YOU are the KING of all KINGS. YOU are the KING of every-
thing. Without love, without YOU, what's this conundrum
world to do? Without the love of YOU insanity builds.
Greed strikes at those who choose the world.
Let them blame the rain.

Oh my LORD, YOU are the KING of YOUR domain. I know who
YOU are. YOU are my KING. I know it's life that YOU bring.
My soul belongs to my KING.
YOU are my KING. Without the life YOU gave, without the
souls YOU righteously save. YOU are the
KING of your domain.

Rain, love and knowledge of YOU. Indulge us with YOUR
words of love. Let it be known that you are KING,
YOU are my LORD.
Your grace should take place of all greed and hate. You are
my KING above all everything. I love that YOU are my KING.

Follow Me

I lived for you. I died for you. Someday you will feel, someday you will see. I can set you free. Hear MY voice, take oh child, oh take MY hand; follow me. Take a stand. Trust in ME with all YOUR heart, all your soul. Understand child all about you I already know. Follow ME, follow ME. Take my hand I bared the cross for each and everyone. Put your Faith in ME, for I am GOD'S SON.

Follow ME, I will lead the way. Know this, I will be back someday. I paid a price for all. I shed my blood. Listen and hear my call. Follow ME, I am the way. Follow ME, trust and obey. Trust ME for victory. Take MY hand child, I will allow you to see the only way. Take MY hand,
I will set you free.

Think Of You

When I close my eyes I see you. When I open them again
you appear. Even though I can't see you, I can feel you near.
It is so much pain and sorrow without you now. I know
I must go on some way, some how. You will always be a
part of me as long as I live. I have so much love that I am
willing to give.

I know that you are in Heaven and you are at peace with
your soul. I know that doing GOD'S work and making
Heaven my permanent residence is my goal. My goal I fight
for and strive for. And I just know that when I get there I
will feel your presence.

I know that Heaven is forever, right now we are all on
borrowed time. I can't wait for that moment but I really do
not have that choice. I just know that when I get there I will
be in awe and finally rejoice.

Into The Fire

There is way too much hate, people lacking fate. Where does it lead? What's it all for? It's getting hot in here. Oh please someone open the door. If JESUS is not your way and along time ago you just pushed HIM away. I got news for you: it's about to get hot. Satan is preparing a place for you ready or not. Tell me, tell me are you ready? Are you? Is that your desire? Well He's waiting and now you're just anticipating.

Well you chose this way. You kept JESUS at bay. Today is your day. Tell me is it your desire? Well it's time for you to burn into the fire. There are very evil crimes that others do. In the grand scheme of things GOD only knows what's true. Too bad, too little, too late, kiss your soul good bye, it's being burned at the stake. A lesson learned. Was It worth it? Into the fire you just burn and burn.

I know that JESUS is real. Heaven is calling me. I know because my heart and soul can feel. I know, I know my GOD is real. My GOD is real, HE is real.

Heal My Soul

There are one's you miss each and everyday. Let the good overcome and sweep the bad away. Live every moment like it is your last. Leave yesterday in the past.

Memories will live forever more in your heart. Embrace every morsel. Today, oh today is a whole new start. Hear my cry, heal my heart. Heal my soul. Oh please wrap your wings around me and never let me go. Heal my heart, heal my soul, show me light, guide me, oh LORD. Tell me which way to go.

It is heart wrenching to know that you have lost a loved one so close to your heart. You get the notion to ask why? You get lost and you just do not know where to start.

Crashing into all obstacles in the way. Swallowing your tears and nothing positive to say. Come back, come back to me. Oh please don't leave me.

You hurt all over inside and out. You just want to let go scream and shout. You think of blame, you ponder it a lot. Life is short, relish what you've got. Hear my cry, heal my soul. Let YOUR love in my heart overflow. Oh don't ever let me go. Heal, oh heal my soul.

Every Teardrop

A broken heart requests YOUR love. A wondering indecisive soul is crying out to YOU, and YOU alone. If only every soul YOU died for felt the same way and gave back to YOU the endless salvation someday.

With every hint of doubt and any shred of hope YOU catch every teardrop that fall from our eyes. YOU dry every teardrop in our lives. JESUS, my LORD, I want more. I want more of YOU, JESUS CHRIST. Any element of YOU is just not enough.

Every teardrop I cry YOU wipe my eyes, YOU show me love, YOU love the man I am and YOU know who I am to be. Teach me more, my LORD. Guide me more my LORD, let me see. YOU are the ONE I follow anytime YOU wipe away every teardrop from me.

Forgive Me

I know in my heart of hearts that I am not a perfect man. I
slip, I fall. Please forgive me LORD, I know you understand.
Give me more of YOU, YOUR love everyday. Let me see clear
now, only YOU know the way.

Oh forgive me, I am here on my knees. Please LORD, forgive
me, I am here to repent asking YOU, LORD to set me free.
Forgive me.

JESUS only YOU know everyone inside and out. Our heart, our
souls what we really are about. Forgive me, oh all the way.
Oh I say forgive me, set me free.

A Prayer To All

Dear HEAVENLY FATHER, oh FATHER hear these words I say.
Oh I pray to YOU. This world needs YOU more than ever. Right
now embrace us in YOUR arms. Deliver us
from all the harm.

Open every eye, open every soul. Oh FATHER show; let the
whole world know. That JESUS, to journey to Heaven, we
must put others first. We are not alone. For every situation
in the BIBLE there is a verse. Know that everyone is equal.
We are all the same. Live with our souls, we are to blame.

Prayers to all, oh hear our call, hear our cry. Restore our
Faith; oh JESUS for us YOU gave YOUR life. A prayer to all:
come save us all; hear our call.

Taste of Heaven

Drop it, stop it, and let go of your ego. It's not all about you
and everything you're going through. Keep others in mind,
close to your heart. Get a taste of Heaven, spread HIS great
word to all that you can. Get a taste of Heaven.
Be a brand new man.

Spread YOUR great name, oh JESUS we owe YOU love. How
gratifying YOU still remain. I cry for YOU, for all that YOU do.
I know that it's not all about me and everything I'm going
through. It's all about, it's all about YOU.

Who's to Say?

Who's to say? Who's to blame? One seeks love, the other fame. HE sets us free, one by one. Yes only HE, GOD'S only SON. The story is true. Yes every page. Read it all and know HIS name. Who's to say? Who's to blame? One seeks CHRIST, the other glory. How sad it is the same old story.

I think about all that YOU are. In my soul we're never apart. When YOU knew on that day that YOU'D give YOUR life and not refrain, I say to you, oh my LORD, please take me now, I am YOURS. Without you JESUS, I would not be free. Thank You LORD. Hear my plea.

Ledge

Standing on a slippery edge, foolishly glancing down.
Everything my eyes encounter; nothing,
nothing but microdots.

I see no one else around at all. Emotions stretched high, my
Faith declining fast. More and more in disbelief, how much
longer can I last?

My mind sending distorted messages to my heart, drifting I
feel, like the air all around. No soul in sight
everything so profound.

Clinging to my thoughts as jumbled as they are. Suddenly I
feel a warm hand lifting me up safely and there I be.

Tears flowing down, my heart opened wide. Thank You,
now I know my JESUS, why for me YOU died.

YOU saved me. Someday I shall know why. Off that ledge
YOU carried me. Now I see a new life.

I Need You Now

LORD, LORD, LORD, I need YOU. LORD, I need YOU.
LORD, I want YOU. LORD, I crave YOU. LORD,
I need YOU now. Oh how YOU need to know oh how
YOU need to hear. I can feel YOU near, near me now.

JESUS, oh my LORD, I want to, oh LORD to be, just to be with
you. Oh, oh, JESUS I love YOU. I need YOU, I need YOU now.
Every time I pray, oh to YOU night and day, only YOU, oh
JESUS I more than crave. Mighty LORD, I want to praise.
Knowing that YOU can mend it again gives it a new start.

LORD, I want YOU. LORD, I feel, feel you. Oh LORD, I need you,
need you now. LORD, you are so dear I can feel you near. I
just want to tell YOU, dear LORD, how and what you mean to
me, every word. Oh my heart just feels ripped apart.

LORD, I want YOU, oh LORD, I need YOU. I need YOU now. I
need YOU now, I need YOU now. Oh I need YOU now, now,
now. Oh I need YOU now. I need YOU, I need YOU,
I need YOU now.

Blindsided

Don't you ever feel blindsided, hit so hard, left for dead?
Don't you ever feel blindsided? Mouth full of questions,
heart full of regrets? Have you ever felt so empty? Like an
upside down glass that sits on a shelf? Have you ever felt
so worthless, ashamed of the world including yourself?

Yeah, yeah blindsided feels like there's nowhere to turn, too
much to learn, no place to go. All particles of life passing
by with nothing to show.

I can change and the world can too. Once you've been
blindsided doesn't mean you're through. JESUS was beat
front to back. With everything to rip his flesh and cut no
slack. HE was blindsided again and again. HE did it all, all
for our sins.

No Love Without Me

Do you know? Have you heard? Do you remember? Can you concur? Do you want to fly across the sky? Go through the golden gates forever to reside? I died for you inside and out; your sins your soul without a doubt. Do you remember? Have you heard? I love you child. I'm JESUS believe every word.

Without ME, Heaven would not be reachable. Without ME the words I give would be unteachable. Only tears of fear and loss would be. No love without ME. Hearts would be empty, souls in captivity. Hate would be everywhere. No love without ME. I gave up my life for souls to be free. Do you concur? No love without ME, no love without ME.

For those that do not believe they shall soon see, I am the only way to victory.

Everything

Hold on to what you have. Hold on to everything. Be
thankful for, oh count your blessings. You're alive for this
moment for this day, do not waste It.

Glorify HIS name for HE is, HE is our everything, HE is our
everything. Our air, our life HE is our day, our night. Each
one of us has a gift. Find it, use it well. Each one of us has
a story to tell. Sometimes credit is taken where it's not due.
All belongs to YOU. Oh my gracious GOD, I owe everything,
my life take it too. I owe everything,
everything to YOU, Thank You.

Thank You GOD for the air I breathe. Thank You for the soul
I received.

Letters In The Sky

Half asleep receiving a message from YOU. Oh how intense
it made me feel. There's absolutely no doubt in my heart,
my mind that YOU are real. There will come a day with truth
and remorse. This whole world will be infested with wars.
There will come a day with all destruction and demise.
When all will look up and see the truth up high. When all
will be, when the Truth will reveal HIMSELF. All will, will
finally see the letters in the sky. Even the lost souls will not
deny. For all they will see and feel the letters in the sky.

The truth of YOU will be read by all, even the blind.
Everyone will encounter the sign sent from YOU. All will
witness YOUR words and doubt not for they are true. Some
will flee with fright, some will glow and sing. All followers
know that YOU are everything; Oh there will come a day
where no one will deny. For they will see the letters
embedded in the sky. YOUR letters in the sky.

Run Through Fire

I look at my life, frame-by-frame, still-by-still. YOU give all YOU have to comfort and save. YOU never let up. YOUR love is here to stay.

I would run through fire, I would race through time. I see YOUR light. I would run through fire to be by YOUR side.

I look at my life and I see YOU. I feel YOUR love for me; I would run through fire, oh through fire to be by YOUR side. I would run through fire just to see and I would run through fire just to be. I would run through time, I would run through fire. I would race through time, through fire for YOU. I would run through fire, fire.

Oh JESUS, oh for YOU, I would run through fire, oh through fire. I see YOUR light.

Raindrops

I call out to YOU; I'm about to drown. I call out to YOU,
when life is like raindrops. I keep falling down, I keep
falling down. Oh does it ever cease, oh even end? I'm
counting on a miracle or even a friend.
Life is like a letter on a path, on its way. YOU'RE the only
one who, YOU'RE the only ONE that's so true.

YOU send me YOUR grace, YOUR love. All to be treasured, all
sifts from above. Life sometimes can be a bit too much. It
can drift away, evaporate with a single touch.

I call out to YOU. I'm about to drown. I call out to YOU
when life is like raindrops I keep falling down. It's like
slow motion, yet I still plunge to the ground. Oh please stop
the raindrops. Let me fall no more. Will YOU then end the
storm? Oh will YOU protect me from the storm?

Lord Of My Soul

If there is one true love that I believe in with everything, I
feel everything in me, there's never a doubt in my heart the
place I wish to go. I won't lose sight oh LORD of my soul.
My precious LORD, I surrender to YOU, YOU'RE all that I know.

I surrender, oh LORD of my soul. Everything YOU stand for
and every drop of YOUR blood, my life is in YOUR graceful
hands; never know what will unfold.

There's never a doubt in my heart the place I wish to go. I
won't lose sight, oh LORD of my soul, the place I wish to go.
Rest in Heaven oh, oh JESUS, YOU'RE the only ONE I love. YOU
oh, oh JESUS, LORD of my soul and I surrender.

I want YOU to know that YOU are, YOU are LORD of my soul.
Oh, oh yeah, LORD of my soul, my soul. There is only one
place I wish, I'm ready to go; take, take my soul.

The Purchase

Oh LORD when I feel so worn down and so distraught. I look
to the sky and I, Thank You for the purchase that YOU bought.
It has me doubt 'n at times. Well look at all the world's
sins and crimes. Yet YOU seem to never empty YOURSELF of
forgiveness and love. YOU supply us with
all that is required.

For it is YOU my faithful JESUS that we should only desire. I
Thank You with all that I have with the purchase, oh on that
rainy day. Oh I want to say Thank You JESUS, no one can tear
that away. YOUR love forever it carries far and wide. Man
we must sigh and swallow our selfish pride.

Must we never forget what took place. We cringe instead of
actually picturing HIS bloody face. We are the purchase no
tags here. Let us not forget JESUS and all his tears.

It's sad to see

It's about time; I've got to stop. Man this world's gone
crazy I'm about to blow my top. Oh how this world let's
just say it hasn't taken a turn for the best. I see and taste
everyday. It's sad to see. JESUS did you die for all to set free?
Was it all up to YOU, YOUR destiny? To be mounted on
that cross? To mend the broken and seek out the lost? YOU
gave up YOUR life so free so willingly for me, for all. Now
look at all this misery. Oh it's sad to see.

FATHER, oh JESUS, YOU are the one to be. I want to walk like
YOU. I'm tired of being mediocrity. I am not even close to
being perfect and it's plain to see. I know I give my all, oh
to YOU. It's sad to see more than hard to digest. Forgive me
FATHER for my sins to YOU I confess.

Oh what a kaleidoscope this place has become. It's sad to
SEE, it's sad to see. YOUR tears, YOUR heart, oh it pains me.
YOUR tears YOUR heart, oh it pains me. Now it's
just too sad to see.

Wake up Call

So you think departing from our CHRIST is the only direction
to go. Well that hurts more than you will ever know.
You are not too late, not at all. For our gracious JESUS took
the ultimate fall. Just listen with your heart. Stop creating
so many walls. When you feel like there's no place to go,
nowhere at all, listen to your heart. Oh do you
hear that wakeup call?

Wake up, shape up, walls are constructed to fall. When it
comes to our MASTER, HE can do it all.

Do you hear HIS whisper? Do you hear your wake up call?
HE knows everyone inside and out. When your name is
called stand up and shout. There is today and perhaps that's
all. Listen to your heart. Remember anytime you stumble
and fall HE will always pick us up and
carry us over any wall.

One stipulation for any occasion. Listen with your heart,
listen for your wake up call. HE loves everyone everywhere.
HE loves us all. Believe in HIM everyday and listen
for your wakeup call. We are here now but not evident to
stay. Remember all that HE did; drop and pray.

I Shall Always

I will always pray and I will always say that I love YOU. I will always rave about YOU. YOU will always stay until the end to get me through. I shall always worship YOU until the day that I die. I shall always call YOUR name and never hide. I shall always swallow my pride dear JESUS CHRIST. I will always walk where YOU'VE been and I will, I shall always repent for my sins.

Don't want to tread down that road again. I will always rave about YOU evermore. I shall always call YOUR name, oh my LORD. I shall always love and praise YOU everyday. When I think of YOU I know that everything will be ok. I shall always praise YOUR name.

Change Of Pace

Stop me if you've heard this one before, you're not a thing
without JESUS. HE'S the one you need to adore. HE'S every-
thing and more. Radiant with love and so much more.

Everyone and everything can use a little change. Maybe
we all need a change of pace. HE'S just not my LORD. HE
oversees all. Everyone can use a change now and then. You,
your life it all belongs to HIM.

A change of pace, fill in a different space. Something
new, another start; hand in hand time to embark. When in
HIS light shimmering with love remember all will change
maybe we all need the scenery to change.

New footsteps to trace, a new world, a change of pace.
A world of JESUS, a change of pace. Let's change now,
why not today? A whole new makeover with a whole new
change, change of pace.

Two Clouds Above Seven

To all Angels up in Heaven and all around: you have yet
another name, miracle, oh I love the sound. Some claim
they've seen you, others in disbelief. I know you exist this
I can conceive.

When tragedy is about to strike GOD sends you here to
make things right. Sometimes you help save a life or two,
whatever GOD allows you to do. GOD has HIS own ways.
GOD has HIS own plan. When people stay or if they go HE
sends you to help someone understand. Only HE knows
when someone is going to that place. Two clouds above
seven. Oh to that blissful place called Heaven,
two clouds above seven.

Another Rainbow, Another Storm

On the inside looking out, tell me what this life is all about. We all have our share of questions and way too many doubts. After all the clouds turn gray. It's just another rainy day. Another rainbow, oh another storm that's the forecast today. You've been informed.

Would you rather have the sunshine all sweltering day? Or would you have some raindrops fall, fall down on your face? Would you make the wind calmly blow the rain away? You have been informed today's forecast, oh another rainbow, another Storm.

On the inside looking out, oh FATHER, YOU exist. YOU'RE what life is all about. Tell me something and answer true, Without a rainbow after a storm oh what would you do? A promise to me and a promise to you.

Let Go of Yesterday

Let me, my heart be as one. I don't want to be another soul on the run. I look forward straight to YOU. The past can be a glimmering virtue, an aspect I find. My life leading to YOU in every way. I see myself free of pain.

I want to let go of yesterday. I want a new path, somewhere new. All I want is YOU. When I look back even when I know I 'm not a perfect person, the past I shouldn't go. I want to let go of yesterday. I want a new path, somewhere new.

My past I will not hang on to. All I want is YOUR love, all I want is YOU. And I will let go of yesterday, I look forward Straight to YOU. Yesterday, oh yesterday is over, I look forward straight to YOU, to YOU. All I want is YOU.

JESUS, oh JESUS, I want YOU.

Is It Enough?

What can I do? What can I do for YOU? To love YOU, is it
merely enough to have Faith in YOU, oh LORD? To love, to
love YOU with all my soul, is it enough even
though everything YOU do?

Is my life equal to YOURS? Does my Faith negate YOUR life?
Is it enough? Is it worth YOUR strife? A pure man YOU were
when YOU outlined the solid path. Is it enough?

Am I worth YOUR past?

Time on this unsettled earth won't last. My love for THEE, is
it enough, my Faith for YOU from my soul? And so I go forth
is it enough? Am I enough for YOUR love? Are we enough
when SAVIOR for all souls sought us out?

All my love simply poured out to YOU. Is it enough for
everything YOU'VE gone through?

Don't Turn Back

Hey, hey I know what you are going through. Hey child
please put that gun away. I know what you plan to do.
I know your pain. I also feel it too. I know you are full
of doubt and hurt. I know child you blame yourself and
now you feel like dirt. Don't turn back. Life does not last
forever. I am your way out, I am your shelter.

I am your tears, your heart, your soul, trust in me child. I
know of a place you can go. I will take you there some day.
I will ease your pain. I will chase your heartache away.
Your purpose here now is to believe in me without a doubt.
You are only ten years old. Obey me to the fullest. I then
will show you up in Heaven, streets of gold.
Do not take a life of any kind. For it is not yours it is MINE.

Don't turn back. You can never turn back.

How Much More

What's it going to take to know HIM, to feel HIM, to ask yourself what do I have to give? What's it going take to trust who you can't see? To put your life in the hands of the almighty MAJESTY? What's it going to take to let go?

How much more does JESUS have to do? Was the sacrifice up on that cross not enough for you? How much more does it take for you to have a little Faith? In HIM we live, you have plenty to give. Just let go and grab hold.

A little love lights the way to a field of Faith. How much more does it take for you? What else does the LORD have to pursue? Isn't HE enough to repent and love?

How much more emphasis can I possibly imply? Take my hand let's take a stand, now the choice is up to you. How much more are you willing to do? What's HE worth to you?

Picture Perfect

You see a blurry image until you near closer. Then appears an unspeakable act. It focuses in your mind like a blown up poster. A little girl is getting hit by every word and a few fists. You're at the scene but her cry drifts. I hear her swallow yet still she chokes. I'm quick not to jump, but to judge. I only react just to utter what is the purpose?

Thinking sadly another picture perfect. This, oh how can this take place? Oh GOD, do YOU see the blood on her face? The man with no reply questions why oh why? What was this purpose? Not every picture is perfect. Images racing through my head. One thought, one idea I just wanted this man dead. I paused awhile, judging not the man that was committing the crime. I did not comprehend why HE could let this occur; the ONE who created mankind.

Why? Why? What's HIS purpose? I know only this: no picture Is perfect. I see a pool of red, my heart racing. Thank GOD, I wake up and find myself sitting up in bed.

Every Whisper

When I think of who I am and what I've done in the glory of YOUR name, I often question myself. Doubt settles in, am I still in the race? I go to YOU for guidance, for shelter. Under YOUR ever-loving arms YOU cover me, protect me from all harm. Every whim, every whisper YOU respond with mercy. When it's pitch black YOU shine YOUR light for me. Every cry, every bit of laughter for all of us YOU look after.

An awful catastrophe strikes a place called Louisiana out of the blue. Suddenly they've bonded after everything they owned dissipates. What they have now is their new found Faith. Every cry, every whisper to YOU is never ignored. YOU feel, YOU hear all, my ever loving LORD. I pray for everyone everywhere in this incorrigible existence. Tyranny, irony, we need to stop all this resistance. You, oh mighty JESUS can hear every heart, every whisper every soul. So many are thankful to be alive and they owe all to a MAN I know.

My Song

I'm not a drifter or vagabond. I'm just here to sing my song. Hear my voice, hear it quiet, hear it loud. Knowing our SAVIOR, oh how it makes me proud.

I'm just a messenger with something to say, oh with something to say. I'm just a vessel made of flesh and blood. I am here to worship and serve the ONE above. Oh I will sing HIS praises and glorify HIS great name. I will do everything oh everything it takes. I will sing to HIM every second, every minute.

When it comes to CHRIST there is no limit. I'm just a humble servant at YOUR every will. I know one thing YOUR love I do feel. I feel YOU all around me, oh everywhere. If everyone just took a second and showed that they really cared. Life would be less full of doubt. Just put your Faith in JESUS and it will all work out. So here I am to sing my song whatever, ever it takes. No matter how long I will simply sing this song.

Oh GOD this is my song hear it true. This is my song from my heart. It is all for YOU. Yeah it is all, it is all for YOU.

Thinking About You

Thinking about all that YOU are. Thinking about the next
falling star. Thinking about all that YOU do, oh I'm thinking,
thinking about YOU. Thinking about YOU, YOU are my GOD, my
CREATOR too. Think about YOU all the time, oh GOD YOU'RE
always on my mind. No matter where I am, no matter what I
do, I do not stop thinking about YOU.
Oh GOD only YOU complete me in all that YOU do. Therefore
YOU are deep in my heart it is all because of YOU. YOU give
my life purpose too. It is great to Honor, to Worship, Praise
YOU. It seems sometimes I haven't a clue. I know one thing
and that is I love YOU.

Morning, noon and night I seek more of YOU. More of YOUR
light to guide the way. I can't stop thinking about YOU. YOU
are the CREATOR the only ONE. I need YOUR help to get YOUR
works done. It is only YOU to see one through.

Oh I'm just here thinking about YOU. There is not one
day that drifts away that I don't relish going to that place,
entering the golden gates of Heaven is what I strive to do.
Oh, oh I'm thinking, I'm thinking about YOU.

All From Heaven

I know and I feel my GOD is alive. HE is real. HE fills my
heart, HE fills my soul all with love. HE restores my Faith
from HIS Heaven above. HE loves each and everyone for
HE created the stars and moon and sun. Also the sky, trees,
water, and land. All for us so please understand.

All from Heaven, HE gave us life HE sacrificed. Without air
we no longer breathe. Without love it is our souls we leave.
GOD is real, HE is alive. There is nothing HE wouldn't do for
you or I. My heart confirms to me that without my GOD, I
would not be. All from Heaven ,HE created big and small, HE
loves and created all.

Glorious Heaven, I want to fly to the sweet by and by. I want
to emerge from the depths of my skin call out to Heaven.
only GOD knows where I've been. My body is a crutch,
a cross I bareth every day. Oh GOD, I pray to YOU come
whisk me away.

All from Heaven, all YOUR love, Thank You for all the Angels
all from above, all from Heaven. All from Heaven my GOD
is real, HE is true. All from Heaven, HE created me and you.

Rock And Soul

I need something solid, a foundation to stand on, I need
something firm, oh someone I can lean on. I can feel that
only YOU can be my rock, only YOU can be my soul. YOU
are the only one, with YOU I do belong.
I will follow, I will go.

There is only ONE, that is YOU. Look at everything YOU
gave. Oh JESUS, look at every soul YOU saved. YOU are my
rock ,yeah you LORD, are my soul. Where YOU leadeth I will
go. Changing water into wine, well that's another story,
perhaps another time. YOU'RE the love. Oh YOU'RE the tears
that should be shared.

Oh to YOU LORD, nothing compares. I can feel that with YOU
I do belong. Oh I can say, I will not stop singing
this song. YOU'RE so very true. YOU'RE my rock, YOU
are my very soul. Without YOU there's nothing I would be;
nothing without the grace of YOU, without the grace of YOU.

Tear for Tear

I speak YOUR name; I call out to YOU. Not just when I know not what to do. JESUS ALMIGHTY, my true SAVIOR all to be. Day and night I call to YOU and YOU listen unto me. You cry my cry, tear for tear. You allow me to see YOU, diminish my fears. With no hesitation YOU sacrificed YOUR life for all mankind.

Love and trust should be flowing through our veins. All skepticism and malice should wash away with the rain. YOU cry my cry, tear for tear. YOU allow me to see not just what's in front of me. YOU cry my cry, tear for tear. Oh Heavenly ONE, YOU diminish my fears.

YOU replenish my soul with love, faith and hope. YOU give me strength abundantly so, YOU steer me from stones that are inevitably thrown. YOU rescue me from all of life's misery. YOU help me to understand many of life's mystery. Tear for tear, YOU cry my cry. Tear for tear, YOU allow me to see not just what's in front of me. Without YOU, well that just isn't reality.

With Honor

I serve YOU with honor, I serve YOU with praise. Fill my heart. Take my hand and lead the way. Oh my LORD JESUS, I am more than so proud to say, YOU are my SAVIOR. With honor I serve YOU, I praise YOU. With honor I praise. Oh YOUR glory it retains, oh how it remains. Deep within my soul with every drop of my blood with honor,
YOU'RE the one I love.

Take me to Heaven with honor, oh take me above. With honor I say to YOU, I lift up my hands, I lift up my voice. Oh with honor I truly rejoice. Oh JESUS, YOU are the light. Won't YOU shine through the night?

YOU are awesome so true to me. Oh with honor, YOU are my MAJESTY. I say YOUR name with honor; I say YOUR name with pride. With honor, oh JESUS CHRIST with YOU I can confide. From YOU there is nothing I can hide. With honor YOUR name is justified. With honor I know YOU are alive.
YOU are alive.

Sacred Blood

YOU remain my hope, my guide for a better place. YOU were the perfect man, which no one can relate. My LORD, my SAVIOR, my MAJESTY; it was YOUR tears, YOUR sacred blood that saved me. Gave me that hope to honor YOUR glory. Now YOU'RE in my soul for eternity. Oh Thank You, FATHER for loving me. Your sacred blood washed me clean, brought me to know YOU my REMORSEFUL KING.

YOU died for our souls and not the world. And it's too bad that most people would die for diamonds and pearls. Shiny things and earthly things. Show me, oh give me a sign. Just to know YOU'RE here. Speak to me, let me hear, show me a sign people often say. Just remember from HIM YOU can never escape.

Signs or not, HE is real. HE is alive. HE saved your soul with HIS sacred blood. HE willingly offered HIS life. Wash me; heal me with YOUR sacred blood. JESUS hear me now. Shower me with YOUR sacred love. YOUR sacred love.

Show Me

I see I see broken hearts in two. I hear I hear shrieks of
sadness too. I feel stranded on the road, abandoned on the
street from time to time. Doubt and fear dance intensely in
my head. Darkness surrounds me from time to time.
I see red.

I open up, please don't shut me out. I need YOU, show me
how not to hurt. Show me how not to hurt, just to
love right now.

Let me know, teach me to finally see. Oh will YOU please
show me? Help the helpless, cure the sick. Let all of us take
that trip. Show me love.

I open up, please don't shut me out. I need YOU, show me
how not to hurt. Just to love right now.

I see broken hearts. I feel oh I feel from time to time, ripped
apart. Show me the way, show, oh show me the way. JESUS,
oh please show me love today, today, today. Show me; let
me see my SAVIOR, show, oh show me.

Teach Me

I want to spread YOUR mighty word. Oh, I want to shed YOUR ever-guiding light, cuz I know what YOU did for me and I know without YOU I no longer conceive anything. I stand in YOUR glory, oh LORD. I stand in YOUR name. I shout and sing, for YOU are the one who keeps me sane.

YOU who holds the reigns, I want to spread YOUR everlasting love. I wish to share with the world YOUR blood. Teach me of YOUR shameless heart LORD. Oh JESUS, let me repent and uncover my scars. Life has a way of derailing man from time to time. Even though we strive to walk that fine thin line.

Instill in me all the love, patience, and guidance that I can receive. Show me, teach me, let me attain only you. Anything else will simply not do. So teach me of YOUR pain, YOUR devotion in retrospect. YOUR blood could fill every ocean deep and wide. That really isn't relevant, cuz with YOU there's nothing to hide.

The Distance

It's astounding to me, always trying to distinguish right from wrong. I do know that YOU represent more than vitality. Let YOUR presence revitalize us all. One more step towards victory. Oh, the journey, the distance between YOU and me, from my heart to YOU one more beat, one more praise, one more prayer too. YOU feel my pain, YOU taste my fear, YOU call my name.

I ask of YOU, to find it in YOUR Sacred Heart to please forgive me. Wipe my slate clean, I choose to go the distance to claim with YOU immortality. I wish for all of mankind to humble themselves, to proudly acknowledge YOU as our LORD KING. Let's merge and go the distance. Let go of all doubt and pray for all persistence.

We are of YOU. Oh, let us pursue this instant. Let us show YOU dignity and go the distance.

There's No Other Way

I've been thinking, yes about YOU. I was just speakin' of
YOU to someone YOU know. I just met the man an hour ago.
Seems like time has ran its course for him in this place.
He's nearing the end. Even though I just met him, I can call
him friend. Soon I know comforting Angels YOU will send.
He's not here to stay, that's the way it is.

Blood and bones, one will run dry, the other just decay. So
hold on to JESUS, make no mistake, there's no other way.
One day overstaying our welcome, well everything will
change. So hold on to JESUS my friend there is no other
way. Blood and bones, one will run dry, the other will only
decay. It is all we have, there is no other way.

One voice will be distracting the other only asking. Will
you let ME guide you? Let ME love you? Are you saved?
Take MY hand, there is no other way.

And blood will run dry, bones will decay. Pick up your
Cross there's no other way. So hold on to JESUS, forever be
changed. JESUS, oh JESUS is the only way. There's no other,
there's no other, no other way.

Through Thick and Thin

It is astounding to me that YOU would even consider my
soul. That YOU have more mercy than anyone I know. JESUS,
I can't even put into words how much YOU mean to me.
Salvation YOU have provided, my chains YOU
have broken free.

Through thick and thin YOU carry me. Oh YOU overflow
with love for me. Through thick and thin YOU died for me.

I know I can feel it in my heart. Yes, I know YOU are never
too far from me. Salvation YOU have provided, my chains
YOU have broken free. Oh my SAVIOR, through thick
and thin YOU carry me.

YOU, my LORD, overflow with love for me. Through thick and
thin YOU died, YOU died, oh through thick and thin YOU died
for me, for me, for me, for me. I can say YOU set me free.
YOUR love, YOUR mercy has set me free.
My soul runs free.

Never ending love

A never-ending job; never have to clock in or out, always
on the fly. Whatever it takes, blood sweat and
tears, always loving care.
A Mother's job is quite clear. She will stop at nothing with
little or no rest with the help and Mercy of
JESUS and only through our LORD.
Any adversary, any test can be overcome. A Mother will
protect a child to the extreme. From a nightmare or a
stranger, anything that shelters a child from danger.

A Mother's instinct consists of what's best for the child
on any given day. Her job is on going. Her warm hugs
and love light the way. Blood, sweat and tears, Mom you
deserve more than one day of recognition out of a year.
Love you, never gonna stop. For you, I Thank GOD.

A Mother

Who sees their born,
Who cries when their child feels torn?

Who loves them no matter what they do?
Who asks GOD to guide and protect them?

The answer is You!

No other but a Mother will and does to this day,
Do all that they can muster for their child all the way.

A Mother,
GOD'S creation what else can I say?

Can I Help You?

Sir can I help you through these harsh and troubled times?
I know that life sometimes can be more than rough. With
GOD'S strength and guidance HE will make us all tough.
When the rain falls all around on the ground don't focus on
the darkness. GOD is shining, shining HIS light for you.

Just follow HIS light to get you through. I see the sign that
you're holding in your hands. I see hunger in your eyes. I
feel the pain upon your face. Nobody is perfect we all make
mistakes. GOD has sent me here for you, so rest
upon HIS mighty wings.

Tell you what I'm gonna do. Take my hand stay and pray
with me. We can't do it on our own. Please
GOD oh please, help this restless soul. Don't give up, call
out HIS name. HE knows your heart. HE will heal your pain.
Don't give up, call out HIS name. Call out HIS name.

Cry Out

When I get up to start the day, I know that my JESUS will light my way. When life, when time, seems to be crushing down oh, oh down on me; I drop to my knees and cry out oh JESUS please. I cry out or I shout out. JESUS will YOU please carry me? Carry me through all the horrible times. YOU are my Answer, please hear my cry.

Oh I trust YOU. Oh please wipe my slate clean. Oh I love YOU. When I cry, out I know that YOU can hear me, always are near me. I cry out or I shout out.
JESUS will YOU please carry me?
Carry me through all the horrible times. YOU are my Answer, please hear my cry. Oh hear my cry out to YOU. My heart is filled with YOU.

Debt

It is known, said to be true, swallow this: JESUS died for me and HE died for you. HE shed his blood, oh what a loss. He gave HIS life on the bloody cross. HE did not wave, turn back, nor run away. Oh the debt we owe to CHRIST we can never repay, never repay.

Life can be sweet and at time sour, oh so sour. Do not be misled there is evil out there just waiting to devour. To devour our minds, our souls, whatever it may. Grab hold of our lives and choke it away. Oh it pains me each and every day. Please, oh please take my soul. It's a debt, I can never repay.

HE did not wave or turn back, nor run away. Oh the debt we owe to CHRIST we can never repay, never repay. No matter what I do and no matter what I say please forgive me, it's a debt I can never repay.

It is known said to be true JESUS died on that cross for me and you. A debt I must pay somehow some way.

Get Ready

YOU'RE the only one I truly adore. YOU'RE the only one, my heart, my faith YOU fully restore. YOU JESUS are coming again, coming back to us again. Oh LORD, YOU saved us, salvaged us once again.

It is so true to be with our FATHER in Heaven is only, only through YOU. YOUR grace, mercy and love are reasons we seek Heaven above. We all must get ready for the day. We must all repent. Let our past sins drift, drift away.

We were all bought for a price. A price paid in full with HIS blood, HIS life. We owe all to HIM. Oh my sweet JESUS CHRIST.

It is sad and awful at times, just look at this world and all of its crimes. Get ready our battle must begin. Put CHRIST in your heart let go of sin. Let go of sin. We must Glorify CHRIST. Only through HIM this battle we will win.

Greatest Story

Oh JESUS, YOU have let the dead yet live again. YOU have traded YOUR life for our transgressions. Oh JESUS, YOU have healed the sick to be healthy once more; made the blind yet see, see again. YOU have let the lame yet stand again. YOU, oh LORD, shed light on every soul. YOU are the reason, YOU are the greatest story ever to be told.

JESUS, oh LORD, for everything YOU have done; defeated flesh, the battle YOU have won. Teach them, love, faith, and forgiveness are our tools. We keep that to heart, well then we override Satan's evil rules. JESUS, YOU are our BLESSED KING, through all YOUR Glory. Oh, my LORD, YOU are the greatest story.

YOU have let the lame yet stand again. May the blind yet see, see again. YOU, oh LORD, shed light on every soul. YOU are the reason. YOU are the greatest story ever to be told. Your message of wisdom, everything YOU foretold. Oh JESUS, YOU, YOU are the greatest story ever to be told. Greatest story, greatest story ever to be told.

Your Holy Name

Vicariously YOU chose to save every soul. In greatness and divine YOU reveal YOUR faithfulness. YOUR love can never be duplicated it can only be amplified. YOU, my LORD JESUS, for us all were crucified.

I call YOUR Holy Name. I speak to YOU. YOUR love will never change YOUR blood forever embraced. YOU forgive; oh I speak YOUR Holy Name. YOUR blood JESUS, it trickles down like rain. And I forever speak YOUR Holy Name. Every essence of YOUR will; YOU can cure all hearts that ache. YOU can fill that space.

The desire that dwells in everyone. The ONE who teaches to overcome anything that will shatter our souls. Anything that man can't explain, oh JESUS, I speak YOUR Holy Name.

YOUR blood JESUS, it trickles down like rain. Oh the countless souls YOU save today; I wholeheartedly speak YOUR Holy Name.

If You Could

If I were to pray to YOU, oh what would I say to YOU? If I were to lay myself at YOUR feet what would YOU do, oh what would YOU do? If I were to fall on my knees; if I were to tell YOU everything, everything about me. If I were to pray to YOU and tell YOU what I'm going through. I ask what would YOU do, oh what would YOU do?

Would YOU make every bad moment go away? Or would YOU delete one day by day? If YOU could, do YOU think YOU would make all Evil vanish away? If YOU could, do YOU think YOU would save me someday? Would YOU help me fight my fears? If YOU could. If YOU could even wipe away my tears.

If I were to pray to YOU, oh what would I say to YOU? If I were to lay myself at YOUR Mercy what would YOU do? Tell me what would YOU do? Would YOU tell me that YOU forgive me of all my sins? Would YOU tell me that YOU love me regardless of what I've done? If YOU could, would YOU tell me YOUR face I'll see, oh high up above?

My Prayers

Oh JESUS, oh JESUS, I humbly bow my head to THEE. Oh JESUS, my LORD, how quickly this sad world is changing, changing right in front of me. I pray oh Dear LORD, for my fragile heart, for YOUR Holiness, for YOUR Forgiveness. Oh I pray for our children to study YOUR word, YOUR ways. Oh how awesome the world would be if everyone just prayed. Many would rather frown than to smile. Oh my prayer to YOU JESUS is to get everybody out of the depths of denial.

Oh just imagine and show them the Truth that everyone was enlightened by YOUR existence, by YOUR Faithful word. I know that not everyone agrees and I find that absurd. Oh YOUR Holiness, I cry out YOUR name. If everyone would just notice that life is not a game. This is my prayer deep within my soul, just praising YOUR great name. Someday making Heaven, of course that is my goal.

Sing With the Angels

LORD only YOU know who I am. LORD only YOU know my
soul. Oh LORD only YOU know where I am to go. Show me,
teach me, guide me through. Take me on a journey, I wish
to go with YOU. I long to sing with the Angels every passing
day. Give all I have in Heaven, oh take me away.

I crave, oh I ponder at the notion, that on that blissful day
I will fly with YOU over every ocean. Oh, please take me to
that place. I want to sing with the Angels
forever, oh for eternity.

LORD only YOU know who I am. Only YOU know the soul in
me. I want to strive to; oh I want to know YOU more. YOU
are my everything. Up in Heaven with the Angels I wish to
sing. Show me, teach me, guide me through. Only YOU can
save me, only YOU can free me.

I want to sing with the Angels, oh for eternity. Oh, oh for
eternity, set me free, for eternity.

Wake Up

Hear HIS voice, HE is true. HE wants to wrap, to wrap HIS arms around you and embrace you. HE indeed loves us with all HIS might. If you choose to flee from CHRIST, well that's your right. We all have rights this is true. You are here my friend, because of what HE did for you. Keep in mind the unfathomable, excruciating, and unbearable pain that CHRIST went through.

HE gave HIS life for you. Wake up, HE is the Way for you. Wake up, hear what I say. Wake up, we are not here to Stay. Wake up, there's judgment day. If you're for our LORD JESUS, get in line. But if you're for the beast well, you're out of time.

We must follow CHRIST, our GRACIOUS SAVIOR. For HE is my Salvation. We shall not waver. HE indeed loves us with all HIS might. If you choose to flee from CHRIST, well that's your right.

We All Need

Sometimes, some days we all need a little more. Some days we all question, wonder what's in store. You can try to deny it. Sometimes we just need more. More Love, more Strength, more Hope, and more Faith. We all need more on any given day. We all need JESUS to clear the way. You can try to conceal it, never want to reveal it. Or you can accept it and admit it. We all need HIM more and more. HE holds our future, our dreams, forever more.

We all need to have a lot more, more knowledge of HIM to win the war. We all need HIM, the most from the highest mountain, from coast to coast. To reach the depths of Heaven only through HIM. I'm speaking of the HOLY GHOST. The love of JESUS, we need refilled day and night. HE is the way, oh HE restores life.

We need more Love, more Strength, more Hope, and more Faith. We all need more on any given day. We all need JESUS to clear the way. We need HIM, we need HIM so. To find HIM, is to not let HIM go.

Do You Know My Name?

Deep within your soul, I am there. Every step you make,
the journey you stride to never fret. Lost one never forget,
always I am with you. MY light it shines,
oh it shines for you.

Shadows in the dark just wallowing away. One glimpse,
one glimmer, one talk with ME you will never be the same.
Do you know MY name? Can you feel MY blood drip from
the cross? Feel MY hands reach for the lost? Do you hear
my voice, to ease your pain? Forevermore do you know
MY name? Must you forget or put ME on hold? Make no
mistake, I live in your soul.

Can you hear MY voice? Can you feel tears from the sky
when you're weak or just want to pray? I live in you. Do
you know MY name? Deep within your soul I am there. I am your
SAVIOR, for I
am everywhere.

Whirlwinds and Miracles

Whirlwinds and miracles that's what life consists of.
Rainbows and darkness profoundly so. It's what concretely
remains, what you sadly have to lose doesn't compare to
everything our SAVIOR permits us to gain.

Love is what HE stands for. Mercy HE showers on each and
everyone. One prayer, abundant love, give to HIM all of
you, anything less will not do.

Heart wrenching news always about. Angels to the aide of
someone in need of care. Do not lose the sight of Hope, for
one day with HIM we are an heir. When stars fall to form an
empty sky, the sun has served its purpose and all is nigh.
Rainbows in darkness for now they exist. Keep in mind to
HIM we belong. We are HIS. All of mankind do you want
to follow JESUS or be a heartless soul? Lost, distraught,
anguishly be left behind?

On That Day

Although we as flesh all struggle in this sorrowful place, let it be known that there's our LORD that sits at HIS throne. Pure and Holy, I speak of the mighty, who for us wore a Crown of Thorns; bled to death for our sake on that day. Oh on that day YOU my LORD carried our sins away. Let the blind see the truth, YOU let them on that day see YOU.

The cross was not YOUR death for YOU live today. YOUR Love allows others to find their way. On that day hope was grim. Three days later YOU rose again. A miracle they witnessed, a promise fulfilled. Oh GLORIOUS LORD, on that day Faith was restored. YOU are to return once again to take some souls away from sin. When least expecting, someway YOU will return on that day.

Life is A Gift

Some would say that life for them is ordinary. Others
simply state that life for them is well, melancholy. Time
is a gift to prepare us for another place. Far beyond man's
comprehension time is often abused. It is too some a curse.

Another time, another place souls of yours will be blessed,
and Honored just to see YOUR face. Life is a Gift; all for YOU
I carry on. Raise my hands, humble I am. Confident in
knowing YOU have the perfect plan.

Life is a Gift, Precious, passed on by YOU. It can sometimes
be cut short and there is nothing that man can do. A gift
from the sky only limited to what YOU desire us to do. Time
to do YOUR work, to only worship YOU. There is no other
GOD; no one else can do what YOU can do.

Life is a Gift, live the best you possibly can. It may be over
in a second. Your life is in GOD'S hands.

Beyond This Place

A society that fixates on objects for sale. A variety of trails
to venture. One prolific way to journey to, one specific path
that leads. Oh that directs me to YOU.
A heart of this world and a Holy heart devoted to YOU. All
that is Sacred. Everything else is askew. YOU'RE all that
matters in this hollow place and beyond. YOU provide life's
essentials. YOU know what we need.

I want to travel beyond this place. There are numerous
compassionate souls. They give all they have. Join the heart
of hearts, spread HIS word of Love.

As we join together, as we rejoice in HIS name, YOU know
what I need. I will follow YOUR footsteps in haste. I want to
emerge from beyond this place.

Lead me to a deeper Faith. To YOU, beyond this place. Take
me, lead me, beyond this place. It is YOUR name I treasure, I
truly embrace. Oh won't YOU lead me beyond this place.

Claim Your Glory

It's not about me to clarify, it's only YOU. Come reign in
YOUR glory, it's overdue. GOD, we only see what man's eye
will focus on. That's what Faith is all about. It constructs
only what is true. My GOD, gather up YOUR Glory it all
belongs to YOU.

Love, YOU love us all the same. Even when we sin, when
we disgrace YOUR name. A GOD of Love, a GOD of War,
Mercy, and Wrath, even so. Yet YOU'RE ONE in the same.

Rules to live by rules to die by. There's only YOU that I
will serve. A GOD of amazement, engage in us with life and
death. None other like YOU will there ever be.

YOU, ONE GOD, only for me. A GOD of War, a GOD of Mercy,
so claim YOUR Glory and restore our souls.

YOU created man in the image of YOU. Claim YOUR Glory, oh
GOD it's overdue.
HE who lives for YOUR Honor and knows truly that YOU are
GOD, shall remain in YOUR Glory. It's not about me. We are
here to live and die for YOU. Claim YOUR Glory it's overdue.

Sign in Again

Hello, there you are. Take MY hand, please don't be alarmed, you are special and dear. I see you crying, with a tear you can sign your name here. Sign when you're terrified or stricken with laughter. Sign if nothing seems tolerable from beginning to end. Just believe and sign in again.

Sign in again, for your sake, your soul. An answer will be given in HIS time, not your own. We live for HIM, we die for Him, too. Sign your name for JESUS as HE did for you.

If you think your chance has depleted and you are no longer loved, remember this: your name is in HIS blood. Sign, if nothing seems attainable or too dark to see in. Reach out for HIM and sign in again. We are here not for ourselves, but HIM.

To die is to live, oh sign in again. There can never be too many prayers or love. Sometimes we need not to forget we all need to sign in again. Any fragment of discomfort we will endeavor. Do not spare a tear. Faith is what's left, sign your name here, HE'S right here.

Without A Fight

Believe in HIM. HE will Bless you. Faith is pure, it's from
more than the heart. It emerges from the depths of the soul.
A simple subtle life with everything is nothing
without a fight.

Lessons learned, tests endured; to live is to learn. There's
only ONE to say what is right. HE lived a perfect life. I'm
with YOU, JESUS my CHRIST.

I'm not going down without a fight. I'll stand strong all day
and night. I'm not going down without a fight. I stand for
YOU, oh I know YOU'RE by my side.

Every hot wire and every flood, one lesson learned. When
I feel unworthy and unable to stand. I lean on YOU. YOU take
me as I am.

I'm with YOU, JESUS my CHRIST. I'm not going down. I stand
for YOU and I'm not going down without a fight. I know
YOU'RE always by my side I'm not going down
without a fight.

You Bring Light

Memories given straight from YOU. The numbness I guess it
gets in their way. It leads me away from the Truth.
Trembling and quivering I feel when I shut YOU out. Alone
in complete solitaire. A horrible existence not even a hint of
love. Can't feel its presence, it's gone without YOU.

The curtain, it must come down with every wall. With
every unsettling sound YOU bring light to anyone that's lost,
numbness enables darkness to breathe, to shun it out.

YOU bring Light and YOU gave me Life. The curtain must
come down with every brick and every wall, with every
unsettling sound.
YOU, YOU, oh the ONE, who saved me. YOU bring Light with
every glimmer. YOU, YOU save, YOU saved my life.

Hold My Hand

Let ME pick you up, have you fallen? Do you hear ME
callin'? You reiterate your Faith to ME. You will claim
victory, overcome with anything. Withstand every
fragment of misery.

Hold on, hold MY hand. You will be free. Have Hope, have
Faith in ME. I'm the ONE, you can see. So hold on. Let go of
misery.
Hold MY hand, I reach to you. All you really need is ME. I
am the Truth, I cry for the damned. I cure whomever I can.

Believe in ME, oh hold MY hand. Rebuke all Evil here and
now. Pray on your knees and make ME proud.

Let ME pick you up. Have you fallen? Do you hear ME
callin'? You, the way I truly am for you. So take MY hand
and start over anew. Hold MY hand. Reiterate your love, oh
child. I'M speaking to you.

Love and Praise

So here I am, here I stand. GOD, I feel torn to the bone once
in awhile. YOUR Love and Praise, my Faith and Hope,
keep me afloat.
My feet stand firm. Onward I go, to walk another mile. I
hold on to the trust I have in YOU.

At times I'll do for YOU all I can do; I Love and Praise. My
hands to YOU I raise. Hold, hold 'em high. Throw my dark
demons into the blue sky.

Heed my many fears into the air; leave them behind with
all my despair.
So here I am to acknowledge YOU and all that YOU do. Take
my Love and Praise it's all for YOU. If I could locate all the
love we all need between us all. Show me the way I'll
make that call. Send it, send it now.

Shower us with YOUR Love and Praise. Drown, oh drown
out the hate. I want to shed YOUR Light through and through.
Wait not for time. Time never stands still. YOUR Love and
Praise we all must feel. Shower us with what is real.

My Love For You

I'm constantly in deep thought. Emotions arise when I
think about YOU. Tears drop from my face and I know
that, YOU'RE so full of Grace.

My Faith can grow a little stronger and my love for YOU
will never die. My tears for YOU will multiply. YOU'RE my
Serenity, my Sanctuary. YOUR arms open wide. I can picture
in my soul YOU with a smile.

My love for YOU, JESUS will never die. And my love for YOU
I will never hide. My tears for YOU will only multiply.
Honestly YOU are the ONE for me. It was YOU who set me
free. And YOU speak through me. I sing a song
for the ONE who is true.

My love for YOU will never die. And my love for YOU I oh,
oh LORD, I will never hide. I can feel it my tears for YOU
have multiplied.

And I can feel it, my fate. Can YOU seal it? Oh can YOU feel
my love for YOU? I say can YOU feel my love for YOU? Oh
can you feel it? My love for YOU, ahhhh for YOU.

Where's Our Faith?

Sometimes I Just want to go somewhere to get away from
everything and everyone, just to vanish from it all.
Escape reality; flee from this foolish world,
this gloomy place.
I want to levitate. I just want to fly away at will. Sometimes
that's just the way I hurt, the way I feel. I know
at times everyone just wants to get
away from it all.
Fake lives, too many facade forming left and right. JESUS,
YOU see but do we? YOU not only gave up YOUR
life for us, YOU encounter nothing but love
and Glory and Grace.
I have to ask: where's our Faith? Where has it gone to? The
Faith YOU belong to, the cross that YOU clung to. Where's
our Faith? Guide us through.
Reality sets in and it pierces through our skin. It shoots
through every vein. Better look now and pray for
Faith cuz someday we will get away
from this place.

Pray With Me

I bow down to YOU in prayer. For YOU FATHER, I would wash
YOUR feet with no hesitation. No reasons to pause, I would
for YOU finish any task that YOU ask of me.

Come now put JESUS in your heart. You will see, oh HE is of
purity. Oh won't you come pray with me? Come pray with
me. HE is our only security. We are all family, all unity.
Come in awe and pray with me.

I fall at YOUR knees. I pour out my soul, I can't stress
enough all that I feel. I realize that humanity can't
compare to the ONE, to the ONE who set us free.

Come now put JESUS in your heart, you will see. HE is of
purity. Oh won't you come pray with me? Come pray with
me. HE is our only security. We are all family, all unity.
Come in awe and pray with me.

I pour out my soul. LORD, YOU can open our eyes. Oh can
you see? We're all of unity. Come pray, pray with me.

I Am Still Here

I call to you, I comfort your soul even when you doubt.
When you forget about ME and your heart is unclear turn
around, you'll then see ME. I am still here.

Trust MY name. I will never forsake any soul that follows
MY light indeed. You can trust ME.
You can't escape MY voice. Accept ME and be humble.
Rejoice I am still here. Feel ME. Hold MY hand.

Make no mistake I will never forsake those who follow MY
light. Indeed you can count on ME. I won't forget you.
No I will not steer you in the wrong direction. I laid down
MY life won't you follow, oh follow MY light?

I love you, I always will. Come embrace ME. Do not fear. I
will not leave your side. I am still here.

MY light, it shines, oh it shines on your behalf. I'M here to
say I light your path. I gather your tears and I am still here.
I am still here.

Purest Touch

I love YOU so, I won't let YOU go. I just want YOU to know,
oh just to know that I love, love YOU so. Oh LORD, YOU need
to hear. Oh please LORD wipe away my tears.

LORD, I love YOU so very much. Only YOU have the purest
touch. Oh LORD, YOU are mine. YOU are pure and so divine.
YOU are why I am alive. Oh LORD, oh LORD, YOU need to hear.
Oh, please LORD, wipe dry my every tear. Oh LORD, I love YOU
so. I will never, never let YOU go, oh no.

YOU are pure love from the awesome Heavens above. YOUR
FATHER, sent YOU here to help us face our fears. To wipe
away all our tears. I adore YOU so very much. For it is YOU,
oh LORD, with the purest touch, oh LORD
with the purest touch.

Today

What was yesterday is in the past. Live for today like it's
your last. Last rainbow; last smile, last hug; all of the Glory
due to the LORD above. Live for HIM, day and night. Live for
HIM, HE is our Life.

Sing to HIM, call unto HIM. Discard the notion you have
nothing to say. Swallow that fleshly pride and open your
heart today. Flesh will wither away; our souls will ever
remain. It is HE that allows us each breath to take.

Can't stop or rewind, or make time come to a halt. Stop,
put down the blame when time seems most unbearable. At
times it's no ones fault.

Sing to HIM, call unto HIM, live for today. Let HIM take over,
let HIM lead the way. Today is what there is. Today is what
we have. Do not treat life like it's just another fad. Hey,
hey, hey we are here now let HIM lead us, do not push JESUS
away. The past is over, tomorrow is not promised. All we
have is today, today, today.

To Serve You

JESUS oh JESUS, I jump at the chance to Praise YOU. I cherish the time to love YOU. I just want to do my part. Spread the Faith and share YOUR love. To tell of YOUR legacy and one day YOU will return from above. I am here to serve YOU. I am here to serve YOU.

It is my Task to serve YOU. It is my Honor to praise YOU, to trust YOU, to love YOU. YOU bought me with a price I clearly see. I am here to serve YOU, oh YOUR MAJESTY. I am here to serve YOU. Do everything I can. I am here to serve YOU. This is who I am. I am here to tell the world of YOU, everything YOU did. YOU gave up YOUR life for all our sins.

To serve YOU day and night, oh to serve, I am here to serve YOU, to serve YOU. It is my love for YOU. That for YOU there is not one thing on this earth that I would not do. I will always serve YOU. I don't know if I deserve to. But I jump at the opportunity to serve YOU. I am here to serve YOU, to serve YOU. It's the least I can do. To serve YOU, to serve YOU. Oh I just want to, I just want to serve YOU. I love YOU, Thank You.

Disappear

I just want to comprehend YOU more. What's concealed in
me, YOU restore. When it seems all like a lost cause Satan
constricts YOU never to pause; and in YOU, He
inserts His claws.

It all seems like an illusion with our hearts in disarray.
Words surfacing from our lips and a glimpse of hope for
YOU to hear. I know others shun YOU, yet YOU still oh
JESUS, YOU will never disappear.

Even at our worst struggles and our worst of fears HE loves
all equally and for us HE will rebuke Satan and HE will
disappear. We have all we can ask and all we really need.
Ask yourself this one question: how much do you love
HIM? Oh yeah, and for HIM are you willing to bleed?

Oh HIS tears sad, even they do not disappear.

You Pulled Me Out

Steppin' out of pure darkness not knowing who YOU were or
even who YOU are. My mind was so clouded, oh so distorted
not knowing YOUR name. I only welcomed negativity and
massive pain. I closed my eyes, my heart to YOU. I shut YOU out.

YOU opened up. YOU showed me how. Out of the darkness
YOU pulled me out. YOU spoke my name so gently. YOU were
so genuine to me. Now I come to know who YOU are and I
know YOUR name. Oh Heavenly FATHER, I am not the same.
Out of harms way YOU pulled me out.
I owe my life to YOU.

So if offended and overwhelmed with complexity turn to our
MIGHTY MAJESTY. Look for the love of light. Let it guide
you; oh pray too. I, Thank You now. YOU loved me; YOU pulled
me out from the dark. Now I know who YOU are.

Only One

I turn on the radio just to hear that our world is crumbling.
How it's in shambles, people are monotonously doubting.
Is JESUS near? Is He real? Why all this Evil HE allows?

If HE has died for us, then why are the malicious killing one
by one? Bullets flying everywhere, taking any life it hits.
Laying down lives of any kind. Oh LORD, YOU see
the misery nationwide.

YOU are the only ONE who can save, who can save each and
every soul. Just look at all the greed this world has to offer.
I don't want any part, let it perish.

It's YOU, YOU'RE all that I cherish. Selfish hearts, selfish
minds, you can't take it with you. Just like everything and
everyone it just dies. Let it be known YOU'RE the only ONE.
Take me HOME.

Will I?

Will I ever see such a Kingdom known as Heaven? Will I
ever encounter YOUR beauty from this world? And only with
YOU for eternity be set free?

Will I ever get it right for once?
For that final everlasting flight?
Will I ever get that chance? Oh that privilege, will
I ever with YOU get to live?

With YOU, everything YOU touch is enhanced. Oh will I
ever get the chance? Will I get to have that sincere luxury?
To share with the Angels a song for YOU?

Take me in flight, reassure me it will turn out right. Ill go
with YOU when I die. So please tell me will I? Oh will I?
Oh please tell me will I?

Time

There is a time, a place for everything. Words to that effect. If that's the case do I really strive to be the best concealing some of life's regrets?

Is there time to Praise YOU? Oh is there enough time to know YOU? Love and hold YOU? Is, oh is there time?

I just want to call out YOUR name, for YOU I want to find. Oh, oh I'm asking is there time?

Earth was created just to be destroyed. Only YOU can fill that void. Full of YOU I raise my voice.

Words I ask of YOU, I ask with my life. Is there time? With YOU, I will not put YOU on hold. With my time I will never let YOU go for mankind. Is, oh is there time?

Borderline

There is a line that corresponds between what's right
and what's wrong. Follow the soothing voice; listen to the
melody in your soul.

Draw the line, watch your step. The cross is yours
and mine. You can't stand firm on the borderline. You can't
hold true to a world of lies. Oh get off the borderline. The
cross is yours and it's mine.

Submit yourself in your life and strive to follow the
Truth. It's time to make that choice.

Draw the line, watch your step the cross is yours and
mine. You can't stand firm on the borderline. You can't hold
true to a world of lies.

Oh get off the borderline. Show your love, hear HIS
melody this time around cuz on the borderline it's just an
unbalanced scale weight of doubt. The cross is yours and
mine. You can't stand firm on the borderline.

Chains Of This World

I've grown tired of being confined to this place of irony; to break free and completely release my soul from the jaws of mutiny. I'm on a quest to reach a place called Heaven. I don't want to reach it alone.

How strong is your will for the LORD? Together we can shatter the chains of this world. HE'S the ONE we can trust and love, we can bust free from the chains that retain us.

Oh follow the Love of JESUS. And nothing can restrain us. This world of havoc also holds many endearing hearts of love. There are souls of Grace preparing themselves for a brand new place. How strong is your will for our LORD? Together we can shatter the chains of this world. I want to be worthy to my LORD.

I've grown tired of being chained to this world. Take me, show me more.

Heaven's Door

A stranger I've been. Now I can see. All eyes on YOU, my soul's been spoken for too. My tranquilities belong to YOU. Day and Night YOU'RE deep within my soul. I find myself approaching Heaven's door.

I'm standing, oh I'm waiting for my KING. It's YOU, it's YOU who holds the key. I walk through the bright streets of gold. Speechless I feel inside the day I leave this world behind. This is the day that the LORD hath made. I will rejoice and be glad in HIM. Oh on that day tears will run, finally run dry.

Standing at Heaven's door, more than determined to step inside. I find myself approaching Heaven's door. I'm standing, oh I'm waiting for my KING. It's YOU, it's YOU, my LORD who holds the key.

Steppin' through Heaven's door, the day this world doesn't matter anymore. The day we all enter Heaven's door. Oh that day, oh that day we should all strive for. Imagine walking through Heaven's door, oh, oh Heaven's door.

In Plain Sight

Too many minds, not near enough heart. Some glad day this place will stand no more. It will be ripped apart. Time is nearing the end. It could even be that day, right now, I can see now.

Wow, what a vivid vision. Some who have never read a BIBLE will utter words while flipping to the first page. Maybe at that time they will show a hint of Faith. On the other hand it could be too little too late. Only GOD knows what lies ahead and waits.

The armor is in plain sight. We do not have to wait 'til dawn. Reach out and grab it. Now is the time to put it on. JESUS fits everyone. Remember after all HE always will remain GOD'S only SON.

Our armor is right in plain sight. Put it on and join the fight. The armor of JESUS has always been in plain sight.

End Of Days

Pandemonium hits the streets, darkness closes in. It has
begun. The worthy YOU will keep. The unholy will fall and
weep. Time will tell, uncover the foil of the earth.

When that time presents itself, what are you really worth?
The dark will close in. The light will be obsolete. The end
of days will come. Dream of a civil way. HIS wrath will
tremble the earth. The end of days are near.

In the grand scheme of things, what are you really worth?
HE is our CREATOR, MENTOR, and our LIFE for me and you.

The end of days are nearing. What do you plan to do?
Loved ones, family on a place called earth, the journey
continues HE is asking, calling you.

Set up and stand your ground. Fight for our KING. End of
days are to begin. This time on earth has to end. Another
journey to begin.

Ticket To Heaven

Oh if I had a ticket, a ticket to Heaven. I believe that's why we're here. I know that I am ready and there's nothing, nothing to fear. Oh, oh the world should know that we are not here forever. That some day we will all vanish and our flesh will be no more.

That's right we all will be judged for our actions and GOD will settle the score. We all need to Pray and have Faith each and everyday. Carry out the race and do it God's way. No one is perfect, we all stumble and fall. We just need a little help, if we want to finish at all.

So please let me acquire what I deeply desire. I need and want that ticket to take me higher. Yeah. We all need to take more than a glimpse in the mirror and ask ourselves, Do I like the image staring back at me? Well do you? You can change. That ticket is waiting for You and me, you and me, you and me. Oh, oh for you and me.

Another Enigma

Perplexed people puzzling, isn't it? Too many forks in
this road, what a treacherous trip. Cuz when it comes right
down, right down to it. It's all just another enigma. Too
confusing to put it all in a box. Can't send it away, gotta own
it today. Puzzled gestures at a twist of a cube. So you see or
do you really. Like I state over and over. In this place of
forgiveness and love and it's a place of hate, poison and
dread.

Another enigma stirring in the blackest of nights. On
the way another day of. Can't really say cuz it's the
unknown, and it's calling out in every direction. It's got us
tied up in every way. Another enigma twisting minds,
And binding our hearts.

Blinding our eyes and locking up our morals.
Too many forks in this road.
In the end though, I prefer to trust the known.
The blood of my LORD. Maybe an enigma at times but HE is
the reason for my life.

CARESS

Caress my heart
Oh LORD, I'm waiting for a sign, only YOU can show.
Caress my heart and guide my soul. My mighty rock, I only
know. Rollin out my Faith, knowing all well what's at stake, I
don't want to be, JESUS. LESS, I'm right here at your side. I
need YOUR caress, I so need it now. Nothing can cleanse my
sins, but YOUR blood.

Only YOUR crimson love will save me. It's only YOU, JESUS,
that can caress and bathe me in YOUR pure Glory. Without
YOU, well it's all just pointless, redundant and meaningless.
That's why I pray for YOUR touch, YOUR Love and Caress.
My SAVIOR, my KING and EVERYTHING in between.
We all need YOUR tender caressing.

LAST CALL

Get on up, let's all go. Do you hear it, oh can you feel it? It's last call for tears and agony. Fires of destruction and killing spree. Last call for shame and pain. It's a new year. Come on, let's go aboard this train. Let me just say oh JESUS, after all HE is our conductor all the way.

Last call to yesterday. Take a deep breath, let CHRIST do the rest on the Salvation train. Ring in a new day, new year and bring on hope, love and tenderness. Oh let us all marinate in forgiveness. May peace blanket us furthermore, cuz on this Salvation train. Night is night and day is day. Rest in HIS comfort. Love HIM forever. Last call for emptiness, last call for it all. Let's go happiness, Let go of hatred and selfishness. It's just a brand-new day. Last call for dreams not coming true. Last call for all your doubts through and through.

On this train, JESUS, oh JESUS. There is nothing HE cannot do. Let's hold on a little longer. Shout out HIS precious name. Oh JESUS, Thank You for this Salvation train. Last call to all of yesterday's storms, Hello to our only Loving LORD.

Shed

Tears may fall and feelings may bottle up.
Hate may boil over. Resentment may strike. Only if you let it.
Not alone, cuz we're not on our own. We shed tears, We
shed hope.

We can shed a little light. All for JESUS CHRIST. In our
everyday battles. In strife sifting through our sorrows. It's the
day of reckoning. It's now our time to fully shine.
We can shed peace. It's in our hearts. It's our DNA. Storms
will always be thrashing, and crashing, shifting our lives
around. We shed tears on our past. It's a day of standing up,
Tomorrows never last. We can shed Hope and Faith. Our
candles burn into the night. We can shed a promise in blood.

The cross of life, we can shed a little light. All for JESUS
CHRIST. Not on our own, cuz we're not alone. Let's stand up,
Let's kneel, bow to the real DEAL. All in the name of
JESUS. Lets shed a little, not alone, never on our own. Tears
may fall. Through Storms we'll fight, let's shed a little light.
All in the PRECIOUS BLOOD of JESUS CHRIST.

Turn it Back

Right behind me on the stained wall. Used to be, a perfectly positioned clock. If time is anchored and harvested just right maybe then you can begin to wind up the hands of precious time. Where would you go? The train is waiting. You choose the track. If you could, would you turn it back?

Spin the hands at your speed. The distance is all yours too. Close your eyes to your once was reality. Charter to another realm. Let go, give some slack. All yours now, turn it back. Time of memories. The best and leave the rest sinking in the sand. Turn it back. You up for a redo. Wish it was that simple too. Your trip halts here, time to snap into now.

Time is not ours to give nor take. Can't turn it back. Not now or any day. We can live and navigate through Grace. You see the clock behind you on the wall, no stain at all.
Perfectly positioned.

Imagine that you really want to turn away that bad. Would you really turn it back?

HOT COALS

There in the midst of a rising flame. Caught between wrong and right. Plenty to take in. Can't let it out but it's all in plain sight. All of my flaws. Not going down that slippery slope. Cuz now I feel like I'm walking on hot coals.

Each careless step I make, this intensity permeates right through me. Pinned to a jagged wall like I'm frozen in time. A broken down soul. Here I am. Still walking on these hot coals. Each step burns to the touch. One foot leading the other, feeling every coal.

This transparent road I'm heading to. Stepping to the unknown. Walking earnestly over hot coals. I want to pick up speed. Why can't I glide over? I know I've got this trap of pride. Too many steps, so far to go over my hot coals.

Time and time again. Feet on fire. Oh where to go. Can't keep on walking recklessly on these hot coals. There's got to be another place reachable for me.

CROSSFIRE

A steel trap, caught in a snare. Covered in a stench of guilt. Holding on to the extent of buyer's remorse. Casting blame and shame at anyone besides me. I will just hide out here in the shade. Not on me, if you're caught in the crossfire. I wash my hands of from this.

Although they remain unclean. I declare it's history. It's in the past. Hey, what about me? Look at all my accomplishments. Join me in the mirror and just admire Me, me me. No fault of mine. I will firmly deny. If you are injured in the crossfire. I think I will just stay out of harms way. Not my style to fizzle out the fire. I project the first shot, then flee to the next.

I blend in with the crowd. I wear havoc like a modified glove. I avoid the walk on the wire. It's just not me. I prefer trying to muddy up positivity. Don't be a hero. Here comes the crossfire, join me, me me in the mirror. You just have to edify and admire. Just picture me as I leave you in the crossfire.

NOTHING SHORT

Fallin apart again I see. Fallin out of Faith in plain sight. Letting go and holding on to your darkest dreams. Evading the fading light. But just let me remind you, you're nothing short of a miracle. In HIS image, HE did mold. He created you and I.

So unbelievable but yet conceivable. You're nothing short of a miracle. Nothing short, not by far. So do you see with your heart. Deep inside your very soul. HE loves you endlessly. Even when you look away. You're still nothing short of a miracle. Won't you keep that in mind, the next time.

The next time you lose Hope and Faith. When you feel like you've lost every bit of GOD'S Grace. HE is so wonderful cuz you're still nothing short of a miracle.

SOUNDS

And it sounds like endless tears. And it sounds like your heart no longer hears. Sounds like you're callin home. Believe this to be true. There is never a time that you're on your own. Not one second, you are not alone. One prayer away.

Footprints in the sand, Bloodstained love. A reminder you're never alone. I prepare a place for you. When I call you Home. It sounds like you thirst for my word. It sounds like you're in and out of the dark. Let ME enlighten you.

I call you my own. Never have I forsaken thee. It sounds like you know. Fight through this storm. It sounds like you're singing my Praises, it sounds like you're wearing burdens and pride. Lift up your hands while I lift up your life. I calm every storm. I live, I died, I rose to give you Hope, love and rest.

And it sounds like through your struggles and cries. One thing remains. I give you everlasting life. Never alone you are. With you I am. It sounds like you're far from HEAVEN. So not true. Each step you take, it sounds like one pair of footsteps. As I carry you through, it sounds like I am right here with you. It sounds like l will never leave you, I know it sounds too good to be true.

My blood speaks the TRUTH. How does that sound to you?

LIGHTING STRIKES AGAIN

It's like heading blindly into traffic. When you pass the rock of ages. For the biggest score. Going out of my way to put myself at bay. Lighting strikes again. This much I'm convinced.

Where there's smoke, you got yourself a fire. And when, when there's Faith, the Sky's in reach, no limitations at all. Start to begin. When lightning strikes again. And when you fall, just remember that beneath it all you're falling into your Faith net. Safe as can be. A simple prayer. A count to ten.

When you consider that lightning strikes again. Where it doesn't rain. How can there be any growth. Without lessons and lightning strikes. It's just a showerless drought. Door to door. A silent shout, ALIVE, on this day. Blood running through. Are you still breathing? Your heart, it's just beating when lightning strikes again. Remember this feeling when lightning strikes again.

www.ingramcontent.com/pod-product-compliance
Lightning Source LLC
Chambersburg PA
CBHW060518130626
46553CB00002B/556